To living lightly!

Maggie Beaubien

LIFE
IS MORE THAN YOUR
YOUR
TO-DO LIST

Blending Business Success
With Personal Satisfaction

Maggie McAuliffe Bedrosian

BCI
PRESS

Rockville, MD

READER RESPONSES
to Maggie's last book:

Some people comment on WHERE they read...

"I keep the book in the extra car I have in Honolulu for my business trips there. Your book gives me a taste of home when I'm away."   S. H.

"When I want to find your book, I look in my husband's bathroom where he reads it too."   B. S.

"It stays under my bed and I sometimes read it at night."   C. L.

"Things had gotten to be too hectic. I ran away and checked into a hotel overnight. Your book helped me want to come home."   K. H.

Others mention HOW they read...

"As an adrenaline-junkie entrepreneur, I'm ordinarily a speed reader. This is the first book I have savored slowly in a long time."   K. G.

"Sometimes I take a mental vacation just by reading one short passage."   L. W.

And a few mention WHAT IT DOES for them...

"For years my family has been after me to wear my seatbelt. Starting today, I will.   U.S.

"When I read about your dad and the 6¢ King Edward cigar, I remembered what it was like to be a boy and to have a dad."   J. B.

Published by
BCI PRESS
4509 Great Oak Rd.
Rockville, MD 208531948
FAX 3018717225

Library of Congress Cataloging-in-Publication Data

Bedrosian, Margaret McAuliffe, 1942-
     Life is more than your to-do list : blending
business success with personal satisfaction /
Maggie McAuliffe Bedrosian.--1st ed.

p. cm.
ISBN # 1-884798-26-8

1. Success in business   2. Self-realization. I. Title.
HF5386.B43 1955   650.1
                                   QBI94-21311

LCC Card Number 95-075333

© 1995 by Maggie Bedrosian.

Printed in the United States of America
10 9 8 7 6 5 4 3 2

This publication is intended to provide guidance in regard to the
subject matter covered. The author and publisher are not engaged in
rendering legal, financial, psychological, theological or any other
professional service. If such services are desired, seek professional
assistance.

Dedication:

To Marty,

The magnificent peasant
celebrating life
beyond lists

SPECIAL THANKS:

Artwork & Design:
Salvatore Concialdi
Ruth Bielobocky
Bill Egar
Liz McAuliffe Gollen

Editing:
Carolyn Long

Technical & Design Advisors:
Julie Perlmutter
Rob Carr

Inspirations & Input:
Beverly & Tom Rogers, Liz Clist, Alice & John Mennitt,
Jan Zeanah, Kathy Griffin, Fred Shulman, Howard Stein,
Ed Bersoff, Marilynn Bersoff, Jack Hughes, Theda
Parrish, Patricia Woolsey, Jim Ball, Lynne Waymon,
Barbara Hemphill, Leslie Charles & Rob Carr, Sam Horn,
Dewitt Jones, Lynette Sheppard, John Azarro, Greg
Godek, Hilda & Dan Willoth, Korry Hatzes, Cathy Hocker

Colleagues in the Century Club of George Mason University, National Speakers Association, American Society
for Training and Development, Fairfax County Chamber
of Commerce

"Writing Godparents" including Sandy Brown & Rita
McCullough of KIT, Dan Poynter of ParaPub, Judith Briles
of the first National Speakers Association Writers'
Conference, Barnaby & Mary Conrad of the Santa Bar-
bara Writers' Conference, John Tullius of the Maui
Writers Conference, and Stephen Tweed & Elizabeth
Jeffries of the NSA Author's Lab

And my relatives who provide a wealth of material: The
Families McAuliffe, Atanossian, Kennedy, Carpenter,
Cavarocchi, Orlando, Mullins, Reed, Gollen, Buonocore,
Villareal, & Lolandi

Brenda Phillips & Chuck Bedrosian, the next generation

CONTENTS

CHAPTER ONE
A Butterfly on Your Briefcase

CHAPTER TWO
Taste The Moment

CHAPTER THREE
Shape the Meaning

CHAPTER FOUR
Hold The Mission

CHAPTER ONE

A Butterfly On
Your Briefcase

THE FIRST QUESTION

What would you say to a butterfly on your briefcase?

There sits your briefcase, brimming with important work, bright opportunity, welcome responsibility, and draining demands. In one single moment, a butterfly lands on the handle of that briefcase.

Your response to the butterfly would probably change depending on your current mood...

- Back off, butterfly, I'm in a hurry.
- That's nice, now what's my next call?
- Whoa, what a beautiful creature.
- You'd better not be leaving any
  droppings on my good briefcase!

Like you, I would think of similar responses.

Rarely would it occur to me that this butterfly could be a graceful reminder that each passing moment is as fleeting as the temporary perching of the butterfly.

Rarely would I notice that life itself is as fragile and fleeting as that winged visit.

Rarely would it dawn on me that the briefcase will be there, still loaded with work and priorities, long after this moment, this day, this life have flown forever.

Life Is More Than Your To-Do List

Once in a while, though, it's good to take time to think of those things.

That's what this book is about.

HOW BAD IS IT?

Ask yourself how many of these thoughts have occurred to you in the last 24 hours...

- Maybe I should hurry a little faster.
- I'll never get all this done.
- There are too many things on my To-Do list.
- I'm exhausted.
- I'm tense all the time.
- I miss laughing.
- I need to play more.
- If I can just hang on till the weekend...vacation... end of this project...deadline... budget is done.
- These people are driving me crazy.
- Where did the week go?
- Nothing stirs my juices any more.
- I've got to win the lottery—SOON.

If you made a tally mark every time you had a thought like these, would your page look like a drenching rain?

*Instant gratification
isn't fast enough any more.*
Mark Russell

LAMENT

Some days
I'm like a bullet
shot from a 357 magnum.

Hurtling through
an unnoticed present.

Into an unknowable future.

Afraid of that stone wall
at the end.

HOW GOOD CAN IT BE?

How many of these thoughts have occurred to you in the last 24 hours...

- It feels good to breathe free.
- My work is stimulating.
- What a great time to be alive.
- Look at the things I get to do today.
- I wouldn't trade places with anyone.
- I produce focused results with natural ease.
- I laugh a lot.
- This is exactly the life I choose for myself.
- Dark times add depth to my life.
- I'm lucky to be here now.
- Life says what happens, and I say what it means.
- I'm having one of the great days of my life.

If you had a relaxed smile every time you had a thought like these, would your days feel more sunny?

WHERE DO SUCCESS AND SATISFACTION SHOW UP IN DAILY LIFE?

I feel...
    strong,
    full of heart,
    muscular,
    light,
    like a big smile.

    Brain wealthy.

I greet each new day.

My cup overflows.

The present brims;
the future beckons.

I'm on a honeymoon with life
    rich
    lucky
    connected
    content.

THE MOST IMPORTANT QUESTION YOU CAN ASK YOURSELF

Do you believe in rich, relaxed results, the ability to produce quality outcomes with natural ease and joy?

This is the most important question you can ask yourself right now. If you do believe in rich, relaxed results you have the opportunity to create them in your life. If you don't believe in such results, your life will always have a higher proportion of struggle than you might prefer.

Believing in rich, relaxed results doesn't make them happen automatically. But holding the possibility of those results allows you to create them more easily.

Combine your belief with skills, focus, energy and luck and you can truly blend business success with personal satisfaction.

How do you know this is true? Do some original research in your own life. Listen to yourself and to the people around you.

Ask yourself: "How do I feel when I'm feeling really well?" Write down the first 10 words that come to mind.

In asking this question in my seminars I get a wealth of answers. Here are some typical responses:

alert	joyful	energetic
relaxed	happy	satisfied
connected	juicy	loving
loved	needed	rich
not needed	independent	whole
full	content	playful
frisky	happily weary	calm
accomplished	contributing	lucky
focused	reflective	childlike
real	challenged	strong
significant	important	abundant
vibrant	democratic	human
absence of guilt	fulfilled	useful
absence of fear	glad I'm alive	healthy
absence of anxiety		at peace

There are also a few that stand out...tranquil, invincible and my personal favorite, omnipotent.

Three important things to notice about this list:

1. The words fall into 3 general categories vertical words, horizontal words, and freedom words.

Vertical words convey vividness, energy, that upright spirit that wants to conquer Mount Everest. Horizontal words convey serenity, calm, that reflective spirit that flows harmoniously through the day. Freedom words convey the absence of undesirable elements in life; they express relief from burdens.

Play with words of paradox. You may feel really well when you are both relaxed and alert, both playful and focused, both serene and excited, both invincible and frisky. Some people find that the blend of apparent opposites creates dynamic tension that helps them feel vibrantly alive.

2. When you feel the way you just described, you operate at your optimum. You find solutions more easily. You release the emotional traps effortlessly. You draw the most from all your internal resources. You find unexpected support in unlikely places.

It's not that you don't encounter obstacles, but you ease through them skillfully. It's not that you don't face challenges, but you face them hungry to learn what they are offering you. It's not that you don't get fearful or discouraged, but you blast through the fear and come out stronger on the other side.

People say,
> "I'm rich in resources and ready to create results,"
> "Things get in my way and I flow right through them,"
> "When I feel this way, I wouldn't trade places with anyone."
> "I'm like a warm knife slicing through butter. Molecules part for me!"

3. The most significant thing about this list is that you have experienced most of these feelings at different times in your life. Think of that. You have had these feelings before. You can have them again.

You can bring them into your life more consciously on a daily basis and use them to create rich, relaxed results. You have been resourceful and relaxed before, and you have created rich results. You will do it again.

Think about geo-stationery satellites. These satellites serve us every day by staying just above their service area and transmitting communication data we use for telephone, computer and television signals.

They orbit the earth endlessly and effortlessly. Their ease of orbit is not because they are free of external forces. It is precisely because they make the best use of three complimentary forces: gravity holds them in an earthly thrall; speed keeps them in a trajectory; and centrifugal force governs their orbit.

It is not by escaping from the forces affecting them that satellites succeed. It is by blending those forces toward their optimum outcome.

Your blend of success and satisfaction will not come from denying the forces in your life, but from harnessing those forces toward your own optimum outcome.

Remember the most important question.

WHICH IS HEAVIER—A POUND OF COMPUTER OR A POUND OF GOLF CLUBS?

I was sitting in the airport when two business travelers walked by.

"I hate this. They make me carry this heavy laptop computer. But the good news is, I get to bring my golf clubs."

The computer weighed less than 5 pounds, the golf clubs, over 30 pounds.

Weight is relative.

What is the heaviest weight you carry?

Which is worse--being overworked or under-played?

WHO AM I?

My credentials for writing this book are these: I'm alive and operating in the last few years of the last century in the current millennium. I'm a part of a marriage, a family, an extended family, a business, a neighborhood, a spiritual community, a profession, a metropolis, a nation, a world.

I am a part of all these things and I am also apart from all of them. I am alone.

I'm a voracious listener. My senses cross wires —I listen mightily with my eyes and see keenly with my ears. I'm Sherlock Holmes absorbing hundreds of details and assembling them into clues. And the mystery I explore constantly is how to live as fully as possible. I'm a sculptor of words, chipping away at all the blather that isn't a true part of the masterpiece of life.

With my master's degree in communication, I have spent more than 30 years working on how to help people communicate more effectively. My clients are executives and CEO's making important speeches to attract investors, inspire employees, win contracts, influence legislation or lead their industry. They want me to help them get people to listen to them and act on what they say.

The biggest secret I have found in all of that time connects mission and message. When the message you want to send is rooted in your mission in life, people listen. When you also add spark and humor, they listen longer.

Once you are absolutely clear about your mission, you can more easily attract the resources and support for making your unique difference, for creating a legacy.

When you wake each day to a mission and not just an alarm, your life is more than your To-Do list.

Your best results come from linking mission, message, and mirth, and living beyond your To-Do list.

WHO ARE YOU?

You are also alive and operating at the close of a millennium.

You drive over the speed limit, occasionally eat fast foods, don't get enough sleep, wish you could exercise more regularly.

You absorb 75,000 words a day, and the Washington Post says you are bombarded with 700 selling pitches a day. According to Buick, you drive an average of 500 hours a year— that's 10 work weeks of 50-hour weeks, or enough contact hours for 10 college credits.

If you are a woman born between 1960 and 1975, you are likely to have more husbands than children in your lifetime.

You think about your health, your future, your family, opportunities brimming and opportunities lost forever.

You keep trying to catch up with ever-escalating demands. You create systems for keeping track of everything you need to do, and get bogged down in keeping up with your systems.

You sometimes operate on a sleep deficit, a budget deficit, a health deficit, a spirit deficit, a dream deficit.

You blink and another day, week, month, year have disappeared. You say to yourself "It can't be Thanksgiving again so soon."

Your secret mind fantasizes about winning the lottery, but you don't even have time to go out and buy a ticket.

You are sometimes afraid when you wake up at 4 a.m.

You are an imperfect perfectionist about too many things.

You worry that your family/business/unit couldn't get along without you for a month. Or it might be just as frightening to find out that they could.

You don't have time for sex unless you put it on your schedule.

The Secret of the Leaf: Of course, gravity has got us all. The difference is in the dance to earth.

TOP TEN TRAPS

Do you feel caught in the Hurrying Habit?
These are the top 10 symptoms and the results they produce in your life. How many
apply to you?

10. Unrealistic demand for control *results in*
perfectionism.

9. Mistaking opportunities for obligations
results in resentment.

8. Postponing play and relaxation *results in*
increasing tension.

7. Operating within clutter *results in* ineffi-
ciency and frustration.

6. Failure to recognize the finite nature of life
results in taking things for granted.

5. Neglect of self *results in* missed opportunities for growth and depth.

4. Being blinded by business *results in* skewed
priorities.

3. Greed for more, bigger, faster, or "the
best" *results in* envy and obsession.

2. Overlooking the treasure of the moment
results in blindness to life's bounty.

1. Failure to define mission *results in* activity
without aim or purpose.

WHOA!

When you feel smothered, it is time to stop.

When you feel that you are always hurrying it is time to stop.

When you overreact to casual comments or ordinary setbacks it is time to stop.

The best way to know when to take a break is to apply the WHOA test.

**When
Hurry
Overtakes
Awe**

Whenever you forget the amazing gift you have--just to be alive in this day, just to have these challenges, these adventures, these sensations, this weather, these opportunities-- it is time to stop.

It is time to say WHOA.

It is time to reflect on life beyond your To-Do list.

THIS BOOK IS...

Not a blueprint.

Not even full sentences all the time.

Reflections and perceptions.

Not a replacement for professional advice or counseling.

A celebration of complexity, and the peace we can create within it.

Not a retreat from the "real world."
A renewal of what is real in our world.

Lyrics for the dance of grace and gratitude that blesses our best days.

An ounce of renewal is worth a pound of repair.

28 DAYS TO GREATER SUCCESS AND SATISFACTION

Appreciate the paradox.

It seems odd to offer secrets of serenity and spontaneity by giving you a 28-day structure to add to your To-Do list. Yet this can work.

Here's why.
1. A simple structure relieves you of some of the burden. You don't have to do too much too quickly and lose heart because you aren't seeing big changes fast.

2. The short exercises recommended for each day will realistically fit into your already crowded schedule.

3. You choose which exercises to do and which to skip. Maybe you don't want to bake bread or take a bubble bath one day. Do what appeals to you and skip or adapt the rest.

4. Focusing on your goals for 28 days in a row will help you gradually shift awareness in directions that will support sustainable success.

The rest of this chapter explores key ideas that provide the basis for the 28-day program. Chapters 2, 3, and 4 consider three powerful principles for finding greater success and satisfaction. They are:

Chapter 2
TASTE the MOMENT

Chapter 3
SHAPE the MEANING

Chapter 4
 HOLD the MISSION
Each chapter includes one focus a day
   for 7 days. Most days have optional
   exercises.

Chapter 5
STREAMLINE YOUR STRUCTURE
Helps answer the haunting question
   "Now that I have a mission statement,
   do I still have to take out the
   garbage?"

Chapter 6
APPLICATIONS, VARIATIONS
& INSPIRATIONS
Provides glimpses of some of the ideas
   and exercises as they show up in real
   lives. From these small moments you
   see the everyday value or the everyday absence of success and
   satisfaction.

The final section includes a copy of the LIFE
BALANCE INVENTORY which gives you a
success/satisfaction index in the seven zones
of your life.

Finally, I invite you to talk back to me, send your comments, experiences, suggestions and enter our annual contest.

Here's a preview of the 28 Days:

DAY	Week 1 TASTE THE MOMENT	Week 2 SHAPE THE MEANING	Week 3 HOLD THE MISSION	Week 4 STREAM-LINE
1	Take the Key-Lime pie test	Let go of anger, resentment, regret	Sketch a logo	Apply the 411 formula
2	Be here now!	Say it new to see it new	Ask yourself some great questions	Clear the graveyard of choices past
3	Kick the time trap	Revisit cosmic perspective	Write your bumper sticker	Cut clutter
4	Sing the song of senses	Take the Life Balance Inventory	Revisit your gifts from the dark	Consolidate your numbers
5	Thank the tension and let it go	Play with cooperation and control	Select a writer for the rest of your life	Practice the 24-hour rule
6	Let every moment be your microcosm	Revel in small sanities	Describe your legacy	Cut the cord on telesellers
7	Take from each moment according to its gifts...	Picture your year	Create your personal crest	Make friends with "No"

Life Is More Than Your To-Do List

SUCCESS + SATISFACTON = HAPPINESS

*Happiness is the exercise of vital abilities
along lines of excellence
in a life that affords them scope.*
Aristotle

I used to be embarrassed that the words "and the pursuit of happiness" appeared in the Declaration of Independence. I thought those words were too naked, too trivial to be admitted so openly in such a lofty document. It seemed like Attila the Hun signing up for cha-cha lessons.

As time goes by, though, I see that happiness is a much more subtle goal with a loftiness of its own. I see that deeply happy people are enormous contributors within their families, their businesses, their communities. I see that happiness spills over and touches others. I see that full and rich happiness blends both success in the outer world with satisfaction in the inner world.

Success speaks more of accomplishment than of fame, recognition or power. Success is creating desirable results through the highest and best application of your resources toward goals you have freely chosen.

Satisfaction speaks more of fullness, richness and humility than it does of passivity or smugness. Satisfaction is feeling complete, connected, contributing, and content.

Deeply happy people
are
enormous
contributors...

THE MOMENT AS MICROCOSM

Lincoln told us that you are "about as happy as you make up your mind to be."

How happy are you right this minute? Look through the following statements and select the one that best describes how you feel right now.

10 = This is a peak moment in my life. All other moments will be measured in relation to this one.

9 = I'm having one of the great days of my life.

8 = This is a wonderful day.

7 = Most things are going very well.

6 = Things are good.

5 = Some things are fine and others are not so fine.

4 = Things aren't looking so good.

3 = Mom told me there would be days like this.

2 = It could be worse.

1 = It's worse.

Which number would you select right now?
Which number would you have selected at 7 a.m. this morning?
Which at 7 p.m. yesterday?
Which yesterday at this time?
Which would you have picked last weekend?
Which on your last business trip?
Which on your last vacation?

Most people report a pattern. They don't tend to swing dramatically through the numbers. They stay within a range of 3 numbers. For most of us, the moment is a microcosm. Each moment is a reflection of our lives.

This makes sense. Each moment is part of the DNA that combines to make up the body of your life.

The good news is that you don't have to worry about guarantees for the next 50 years! You can improve your life by creating better moments.

The entire story of your life is told every single day.

BLENDING VS BALANCING

So many people focus on "balancing work and home." That creates an image of the scales of justice, one side goes up, while the other goes down, and there are only two variables. I don't know anyone who has only two variables.

Others work on "juggling all the priorities." Again the image is hyperactive. It's a rare juggler who can keep seven items going all at once, yet that's what we try to do day by day.

Rather than thinking of balancing two variables, or juggling an amazing seven, I think of blending all seven.

Like a great tossed salad, we can have them all in the same bowl and season them with our attention. We can mix health, family, finance, career, community, spirit and self and enjoy nourishment and benefit from each one.

HEALTH   CAREER

FAMILY   COMMUNITY

FINANCE   SPIRIT

SELF

WHAT GETS IN THE WAY?

RULES, ASSUMPTIONS AND BLINDERS

Rules are often helpful. Rules called laws keep us from all plowing into each other on the highway. One risk that comes with rules is that they condition us to make assumptions. They encourage us to imagine or assume rules where none exist. This can be dangerous, or at least unproductive.

Here's an experiment a client showed me. Consider these eight words until they make perfect sense as a sequential communication:

TIME FLIES.
I CAN'T.
THEY FLY TOO FAST.

I puzzled over this for a long time. A few people "get it" immediately. Some don't even see the point after it is explained.

Most people assume that the first line is in the format of (Noun, Verb). This can make sense in the sequence until they get to the word "They." Once they switch that structural assumption about the first line to (Verb, Noun) the sequence makes sense.

The stronger your original assumption about the first line, the tougher it is to see the other sequence. This is an optical illusion for the mind. It's also an example of how trapped we can be by assumptions.

6 TYPICAL RULES THAT AREN'T THERE

1. **LIFE IS SERIOUS** Where is your evidence? Where does it say that we are designed to plod our humorless paths to the next paycheck and the next visit to the mall? Is there not ample evidence, in fact, that our very humanity is funny?

Isn't it funny that the mightiest of us all still has daily need of food, water, sleep and bathrooms?   Isn't it funny that no matter how much money you have you still can't hire someone to go through surgery for you?

2. **WORK HARD FOR SUCCESS** Many people who work hard produce only hard work. Many people who work easy produce focused results with natural ease. Bob Kriegel makes a great comment about working hard. "Don't try hard, try easy. A cool and passionate 90% will always beat a tense 110%."

This reminds you to care a lot about producing great results, and also appreciate what you learn from mistakes. So either way, you win. It also invites you to visit your own best successes. Have any of them come from clear focus and the elegant use of resources toward a goal that attracted you magnetically? If it happened even once, it can happen again.

3. **LIFE IS ABOUT "MORE"** Have you ever stopped to define "enough"? Can you ever be

thin enough, rich enough, loved enough, loving enough, smart enough, tall enough, funny enough, happy enough? What is enough square footage in your house, enough horse-power in your car or boat, enough windows in your office, enough trophies on your mantle?

If you have no ideas how much is enough, how will you know when to stop striving? If you don't know how much is enough, how can you add just one more and feel a grand sense of "plenty."

4. **HOLIDAYS ARE FOR FAMILY** This can be a great assumption. Until you hit a snag. Perhaps you've moved to a new area and don't know people yet, or someone in the family died this year and you are struggling about whether to try to do the old traditional thing.

Some friends faced this choice a few years back and the parents and two kids helped serve Thanksgiving dinner at a homeless shelter. They renewed their own sense of thanksgiving and extended their definition of "family."

5. **I SHOULD KEEP BUSINESS CARDS I GET FROM OTHERS** Here is one of the dangerous assumptions that confuses the line between social politeness and business practicality.

Barbara Hemphill, author of TAMING THE PAPER TIGER, has a great solution. When she is processing paper at the end of a conference or meeting she asks herself: "*Do I have this business card because I wanted it or because they wanted me to have it?* " If she wanted it, she files it. If not, it becomes part of the "Art of Wastebasketry."

6. I SHOULD ONLY BUY ONE PAIR OF SCISSORS
This is an assumption based on an old tape in your head from some benighted childhood pattern. A friend in her 50's commented recently: "*I grew up hearing that you only needed one of anything in your house. So time after time I would go from the computer desk to the copy area and get the scissors to do a small task. I would replace them in the desk. Finally it dawned on me that I could have scissors in the copy area. I could have them near the telephone. I could have them at home in a kit for wrapping gifts. I could have 7 pairs of scissors and simplify my tasks. What a liberation!* "

Rules about business cards and scissors don't sound as if they will imprison you in an unfulfilling life. They are subtle limiters that can engrave themselves in your brain without your ever having voted on them. They sneak in some back door and hover menacingly, waiting to sabotage your success and satisfaction.

YOU AND YOUR TO-DO LIST

Some people think that a To-Do list is a necessary part of being alive. Some hate it. Others love it.

One friend confesses, "I sometimes write things on the list that I've already done just for the joy of having items to cross off. It's almost a sensual pleasure!"

Here are some other ways people have described their lists to me:

> It's the tyrant of my time.
> I only use it as an occasional reminder.
> I keep mine on my computer--then cover the computer with notes.
> I use one unified system.
> I have lots of little slips of paper.
> I'd die without my sticky notes.
> I keep one list of all my To-Do lists.
> I'm so compulsive that I have to list time for bathroom, sex, and making my list.
> I never touch one.
> Someone else runs my schedule.
> I have one for work only.
> I have one for nonwork only.
> My format reflects my personality.
> I forget to look at it.
> Once I write it down I can forget it until it requires some action.
> It's the best thing in my day.

I hate it when anyone else tries to impose
their items on my list.
It's the worst thing in my day.

Whatever form of list you currently use, consider the relationship between your list, your
time and your energy.

The Dynamics of Time, Energy, & To-Do

Vision - Pulls me magnetically
toward a desired future

To-Do - Pushes me to
accomplish tasks soon

Today - Priceless time to
be here NOW

Ta-Da - Past accomplishments
that fuel me

Baggage - Past burdens
that weigh me down

MAKING YOUR TA-DA LIST

Your To-Do list focuses on items you are working on. That's great and helpful. Your "Ta-Da" list focuses on accomplishments. That's great and inspirational.

Reflect regularly on what you have contributed, what you have completed, what you have accomplished.

Here's a process you can use weekly, monthly or anytime you are ready for such a review.

1. Reflect on each of the 7 zones of life.
2. Write a phrase or draw an icon for specific accomplishments in each area.
3. Share your list with someone or revel alone in your sense of learning, growing, contributing.

Don't limit yourself to successful completions. Sometimes it is good to celebrate steps in the process. Some things are worth listing just because they are finished, some because they are started, some because you have reached a milestone, some because they have been avoided.

Honor setbacks and failures also, as long as you have grown stronger or wiser because of them.

Here are some typical items people put on Ta-Da lists:

HEALTH   Focus on Vigor

Maintained weight even on vacation
Exercised 22 days this month
Tasted tofu
Watched exercise show on television
Read article on strength training
Practiced deep breathing most mornings
Ate fruit every day
Tested and became horrified to find that
    1/3 of me is fat
Danced barefoot on a beach

CAREER   Focus on being of Value

Completed monthly report
Developed proactive marketing strategy
    for our technical professionals
Served as mentor in the George Mason
    University MBA Program
Spoke on my industry at career day
Called to thank the resigning association
    newsletter editor
Campaigned to enlist a new newsletter
    editor
Completed forms in time to run for
    national office of professional
    organization
Completed over 100 phone calls
Handled payroll pressure without snags

COMMUNITY   Focus on Connection

Gave blood at Red Cross
Helped in Adopt-A-Highway program
Voted
Donated time to United Way Volunteer
    Training Center
Bought holiday gifts at charity event

Attended community concert
Visited sick neighbor at hospital
Took canned goods to church food drive
Donated wool jacket to Work Center
Picked up kids in car pool for a neighbor
Coached girl's soccer team

FAMILY   Focus on Love
Celebrated Brenda's birthday
Breakfast with my sister
Visited the cemetery
Wrote annual letter to stay in touch
Scheduled an extra day on the Atlanta
          business trip to see relatives
Sent 2 special-occasion cards
Bought Christmas gifts for the kids
Hosted family brunch
Called to order special tickets

FINANCE   Focus on Attention
Focused on feeling rich
Noticed the freedom I enjoy because I
          like being frugal
Read article on when to make a new will
Debated long-term housing options
Paid all my bills
Sent out invoices
Planted quarters in phone booths for
          people to find
Scaled back marketing plan due to cash
          crunch
Luxuriated in raspberries for breakfast
          one day
Kept up mortgage payments even after
          being out of work for a while

SPIRIT   **Focus on Thanks**

Worshiped something beyond myself
Stayed aware of my mission in life
Appreciated my daily breath
Wondered again about the turmoil in the
    world
Noticed nature's majesty and beauty
"Looked up in perfect silence at the
    stars"
Took moments every day to glow with
    grace and gratitude
Let spiritual music flow gently into my
    mind
Gave comfort to a friend whose dad is ill

SELF   **Focus on Respect**

Took time alone
Thought about my dreams
Read for fun
Renewed my resources
Listened to library tapes in car
Focused on feeling rich and relaxed
Took a walk in warm rain
Lectured myself for speeding more than
    usual
Got a manicure
Laughed freely
Daydreamed about retirement
Made this list

Individually these are not necessarily life-
changing events. But combined, they are the
small elements that make up our time on
earth. We might as well notice them and
breathe a sigh of accomplishment for all we

do. This can help balance our focus on what we have yet to accomplish on those To-Do lists!

I heard the term "Ta-Da lists" from Lynette Sheppard. Lynette is a health-care training specialist who works with many professionals in wellness and medicine to keep them rich in resources so they are better able to serve patients.

Do you know how to make your spirit smile?

LIVING IN QUADRANT FOUR

*When do you operate with ease and joy and
accomplish exactly what you want?*
Martha Spice

From the moment I heard performance and
productivity specialist, Martha Spice, ask that
question, I was intrigued. I knew that it was
possible to operate with ease and joy because
I knew I had done it some times in the past.

Ask yourself the same questions. How can
you produce focused results with natural
ease? How can you create rich results while
feeling relaxed?

Imagine the bottom line of a grid as a horizontal line from 0 (low) to 10 (high) representing
the amount of tension you hold as you operate to produce results.

Now position a vertical line on the left of the
grid to indicate the quality of what you
accomplish. 0 (low) to 10 (high).

Quadrant 1 (lower left) is **Low Accomplishment, Low Tension**. This is time spent
"vegging out" perhaps in front of the television or doing anything you find mindless yet
moderately enjoyable. People usually think
activity in this quadrant is relaxing, yet they
often feel restless, irritable and generally
drained after spending time here.

This quadrant is symbolized by a snail who doesn't go anywhere much, but can provide minor nourishment as escargot.

Quadrant 2 (lower right) is **Low Accomplishment, High Tension.** This is time wasted in frustration, perhaps when you are stuck in traffic, standing in line or filling out forms you don't see the value of. Much of the anguish in this quadrant comes from feeling out of control, powerless and insignificant.

The symbol is a road runner, constantly hurrying just to stay upright, without getting anywhere.

Quadrant 3 (upper right) is **High Accomplishment, High Tension.** This occurs when you have an incredibly productive day and you look back to see dead bodies strewn in your wake. These are the people you had to burn through to get results. You win in the short term and feel their sabotage or heat down the road. You feel momentarily mighty, yet vulnerable.

The symbol is a pit bull who does everything with unnecessary roughness.

Quadrant 4 (upper left) is **High Accomplishment, Low Tension.** This occurs when you operate in the fullness of your resources. You are focused on a goal worth reaching, you have support and energy for approaching it. Obstacles turn into challenges as your momentum carries you elegantly forward. This is part of why you are here. This is what you are supposed to be doing. This is both a choice and a celebration. Yes, there is effort. Yes, there is exhaustion. But where you are going and how you are getting there feel right. In sports this is called being "in the zone."

The symbol is both a strong, majestic eagle and its graceful cousin, the butterfly.
The more you know about yourself and Quadrant 4, the more often you can visit there. Maybe even live there!

The letters High Accomplishment, Low Tension (HALT) also remind us that this is a way to halt or reduce the unproductive stress that robs you of productivity and threatens your health.

Look over the diagram on the next page to see where you fit. How can you spend more time in Quadrant 4?

THE RELAXED RESULTS QUADRANT

Where are you now?

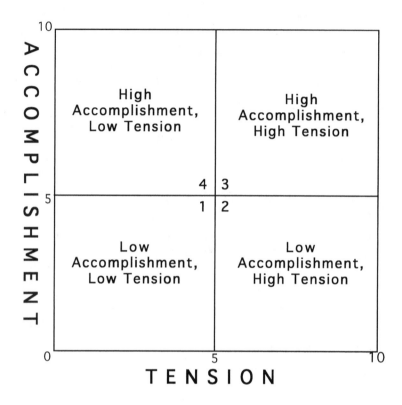

CORNERSTONES REVISITED

These, then, are the cornerstones of this
book:

      Be good to your butterfly
      Blend To-Do with Ta-Da
      Rent some space in Quadrant 4
      Respect your finite resources

CHAPTER TWO

Taste
The Moment

FOCUS OF WEEK ONE

This week's focus is on tasting the moment. Take the time and apply your awareness to suck the juices out of each day as you live it. Revel in the non-renewable treasure of each moment.

After two short selections to set the tone for the week, you'll find seven exercises--one for each day. The exercises for this week heighten your awareness and sense of immediacy.

If you're traveling at the speed of light, what do you use for headlights to show the way?

A SAN FRANCISCO SMILE

I was walking down the street approaching the knife-sharp stone steps of an imposing bank. She came out of the bank—polished, professional, vigorous. She had on the business uniform of charcoal grey suit, white shirt, tie, conservative black pumps. Her dark hair was styled with severe simplicity. Her right hand had a deathgrip on her briefcase. So far she presented a total no-nonsense portrait of a 90's professional. Her left hand gave it all away. In it she held an ice cream cone.

As she juggled the melting ice cream cone with the overstuffed briefcase, she broke into a radiant smile. She was finding a few seconds of holiday inside somber responsibilities.

I laughed as we exchanged amused glances. I wasn't laughing at her so much as I was laughing at myself. How often do I keep that deathgrip on the briefcase when I could as easily be noticing the incredible flavor, texture, temperature, flow, and crunch of the ice cream cone?

TASTE YOUR 3.14 BILLION SECONDS

In your first 100 years you will experience 3.14 billion seconds. No, maybe you will only experience a few thousand. But you will **have** 3.14 billion seconds. How many of those will you slip through on automatic pilot?

It's good that we are not required to stay 100% tremblingly aware of each sensation, each breath, each nonrenewable second of our lives. Imagine being conscious of each strand of clothing on your body, of the level of moisture on your tooth enamel right this second, of the tension in your right shoulder at this moment. Awareness is exhausting.

The National Bureau of Standards in Gaithersburg, Maryland, built an anechoic chamber within their sound testing facility. It is designed to still all echoes so sound can be measured accurately. The chamber is pitch dark, since even light emits sound. After about 40 seconds sealed in a soundless, black chamber you can start to hear your own heart beating. You can hear the blood coursing through your veins. The experience can be frightening. I am usually happy to let my autonomic system operate without my conscious participation.

But it makes me lazy. I turn more and more of my life over to automatic systems. Before long I am forgetting to taste any but the most dramatic moments of my life.

Day 1. TAKE THE KEY-LIME PIE TEST

Assume for one moment that you like key lime pie. You like the piquant tang of sharp sweetness on your tongue. You like the crunch of a perfect crust and the loft and flavor of a dab of whipped cream. Bring your attention fully to this thought for a moment.

Did you feel any sensations? Most people find their mouths watering as they imagine the flavor of the pie. Isn't that amazing? You can sit there holding this book and create an idea so powerful it triggers a salivary response that prepares you for the experience of eating the pie. You can sit there with no pie and have some vivid elements of the experience of eating the pie.

Conversely, you can dine in splendor, eat at the deli, breakfast in the cafeteria, or share dinner with your family and never taste one morsel of food at all. You might as well be shoveling in nutritional cardboard for all you notice.

The difference is awareness. You can have full rich mental adventures even without the physical counterpart. Or you can have physical activity without attention, and experience almost nothing. Now remember the power of blending rich mental awareness and physical experience. These are wonderful times.

Is there anything in your day today you are experiencing as richly as you "tasted" the imaginary key lime pie?

Day 2. BE HERE NOW -- THE MORE I FEEL, THE MORE I FILL

The more I take time and attention to notice the wonders of being alive in this day, the more I fill my storehouse of resources. The more I fill my resources, the better results I create, the more successful and satisfied I am.

Childhood is a time of NOW. Kids stay in the moment. This is why they drive us crazy with repeated questions like "Are we there yet?" Finally we tame them and help them accept time, sequence, delayed gratification. Can we ever recover the time of NOW?

To "be here now" requires that I breathe. So breathe consciously. I once listened to a wonderful audiotape called "The Present Moment," by Thich Nhat Hanh. He speaks with a strong Vietnamese accent, or maybe I listen with a strong American filter. Anyway I listened to the tape several times and enjoyed his simplest of all meditations. The breathing meditation.

I heard him say, "Breathing in, I relax; breathing out, I smile." I practiced this for weeks. It was wonderful. I practiced in traffic, on my walks, at tense moments. Later I listened to his tape again. This time I heard it differently. He said "Breathing in, I release; breathing out, I smile." I think I was meant to hear the "wrong" version. It works wonderfully for me.

We risk turning all our attention over to PAST or FUTURE and forget about NOW.

Life Is More Than Your To-Do List

WHY BABIES CAN GET
WHAT THEY WANT
AND WE CAN'T

Babies want very simple things.
They want to feel:
>   dry
>   full
>   warm
>   safe
>   loved
>   secure
>   challenged.

We want:
>   more money
>   time to do what we want to do
>   a relationship others envy
>   a dropdead body and the wardrobe to
>   match
>   our face on the front page of the *Wall
>   Street Journal*
>   liposuction
>   a flashy car
>   to lose 10 pounds
>   great hair days
>   new computers/toys/tools
>   to win the lottery.

This is another variation on God's joke.
As we grow up we forget to tell ourselves the
truth.

If only we would remember to know.
We want very simple things.

We want to feel:
     dry
     full
     warm
     safe
     loved
     secure
     challenged.

Day 3. KICK THE TIME TRAP

Focusing on the past can be pleasant if you think about accomplishments or happy memories.

More often, though, we review the past to berate ourselves for mistakes, flaws, missed opportunities. Or we think of others with resentment, anger, envy, guilt or regret.

Thinking of the future is good if we are creating a vision so clear and palpable that it magnetically pulls us toward taking appropriate action in the present.

Instead, most of us think that the future is the present, with anxieties. We bring tomorrow into today with concern, fear, worry, inadequacy or mistrust.

Imagine the word NOW being squeezed from the left by a boxing glove labeled REGRET (past) and from the right by a boxing glove labeled FEAR (future).

One of my goals is to have more NOW now. Think about the word NOW

Noticing
Ordinary
Wonders

Think about the times you are present in the moment. What is the confluence of brain and body, of attention and experience when you feel most alive? When does that happen? What are the moments you savor?

Here are some comments from people in my seminars:

    Taking a hot bubble bath

    Sex

    A relaxed dinner with my spouse

    Dancing

    Playing sports

    Cooking in a fragrant kitchen

    Washing my car and playing in the
        soapy water

    Changing a baby

    The sadness of missing my friend who
        died this year

    Laughing out loud

    Slicing carrots and noticing the design in
        each cross section

    Walking my dog

    Savoring the sunshine

    Seeing the light in crystal ice-covered
        branches

    Listening to a freshly-tuned engine

Notice that these do not need to be moments of glory or even of joy. They are ordinary moments to which has been added that special ingredient—awareness.

Give yourself some NOW at three different points today. Once at home, once at work and once in daily operations.

Day 4. SING THE SONG OF SENSES
Notice also that the list for day 3 includes sensory details. We feel more NOW when we revel in sensory input.

FROM FLAT...

You can even turn changing a flat tire into a NOW moment. First you unhook the past (anger at yourself that you didn't prevent this inconvenience). Then you unhook the future (urgency that this will make you late and throw your whole schedule off). A flat tire is a nonnegotiable need. You don't change your circumstance by feeling angry or urgent. The tire is flat. You will do something about it now.

There are alternatives. You can call for help. You can let your appointment know you will be late. You can take a taxi and have the car towed. You can get another ride and deal with this later. In any case, you encounter a moment different from what you expected in your day.

You can say to yourself: "I am rich in alterna- tives." Or "I will fix the tire." If you elect to fix the tire, you have a perfect opportunity for NOW. What smells come out of your trunk? What does it feel like to take out the jack? What sound does the trunk make slamming shut? Do you congratulate yourself for having safety flares to light, and gloves to protect your hands? What happened to make the old tire flat? How does it feel to lift the old tire

off? What's the sound of the jack cranking
down? Do you have a strong sense of accomplishment and self sufficiency in completing
the job?

Admittedly, these would not be most people's
first or automatic reaction. The point is, you
were going to do something anyway. Are you
better off to be cursing the inconvenience,
resenting the time loss, fearing stains on your
clothes, dreading the replacement or repair of
the tire, hating the injustice of the event? Or
are those the very feelings that cause you to
scrape your knuckles, smear your jacket, or
scratch your car.

TO FOOD...

Food is another trigger of sensory music. The
music comes from eating deliberately, tasting
each morsel of broccoli or banana. It often
comes more vividly from cooking and basking
in the textures, temperatures, sounds and
magical aromas of nature's plenty.

Here is a special recipe ...
TAHOUKI'S CHOREG
Armenian Coffee Cake Bread
Here's a recipe designed to nourish the spirit
and the stomach. Assembling, mixing, letting
it rest overnight while you do the same, and
early morning baking are a wonderful way to
greet a special day like any Saturday or a
family holiday or vacation breakfast while
visiting friends. The smells of its baking will
bless your house all day.

Ingredients

Get ready first:

3 sticks of melted butter (3/4 lb.)

3 packets of yeast dissolved in 1/3 cup warm
      water and 1 Tablespoon sugar

Dry ingredients:

5 lbs plain white flour (sifting is good)

2 cups sugar

2 teaspoons baking powder

1 teaspoon salt

2 Tablespoons of Mahleb spice (Available from
      Armenian or middle-eastern store.
      Optional but exquisite!)

Wet ingredients:

12 eggs (beaten)

1 cup peanut oil

1 15-ounce can of evaporated milk

Just before baking:

2 more beaten eggs to brush on top

sesame seeds

The steps:

Melt the butter in small pan, let cool. Dissolve yeast in water and sugar and let rise about 15 minutes while you prepare other ingredients.

In large bowl, mix 12 beaten eggs, all the milk, cooled melted butter, oil, yeast mixture. Stir with a wooden spoon.

In another bowl mix dry ingredients—flour, sugar, baking powder, salt, spice. Blend gently.

Add dry ingredients to liquid ingredients. Use your hands now to finish mixing and knead the dough gently till it pulls away from the side of the bowl. It will also pull away easily from your hands.

It's time for the dough to rest and rise. It will almost double in size while it rises so be sure to have plenty of room in the bowl. You may want to divide your dough into two big bowls and cover each with waxed paper or plastic wrap. Let the dough sit in a warm place over-night (7-8 hours). I cover mine with a blanket to keep it cozy.

Margaret Krikorian and Anne Atanosian, the Choreg experts, tell me that I kill the yeast by letting it rise so long. They recommend that you let the dough rise 3-4 hours in a warm place. Then form dough into loaves and let rise again for an hour; then bake. Their bread is lighter, but I love to wake up to the baking. Try it either way!

After a good night's sleep, go to your kitchen and behold the sight! If things went right you will have a huge mass of light, airy dough. If not, you blew it and you're out $15 in ingredi-ents! (This is a very forgiving recipe, I once forgot the sugar till the end of the kneading step and the resulting bread was still wonder-ful.) Preheat the oven to 350 degrees and grease several flat pans or cookie sheets.

This is another great time. You can work the dough on a floured countertop, or in the air with just your hands, like they do in pizza commercials. Pinch off a glob of dough larger than a golfball and smaller than a baseball. Shape it gently into a rope 10-12" long. Curl the rope into a patty about 5-6" round. Or crisscross three ropes into a braid. Ropes can also be shaped into a heart, initial or other favorite shapes. Bread expands again during baking so leave room around each item.

Brush the uncooked patty or braid with beaten egg and sprinkle with sesame seeds. Bake for about 25-30 minutes until golden brown. This recipe makes about six large braided loaves or about a dozen patties.

This bread is delicious as coffee cake, toast, french toast. It's especially good with apple butter. Enjoy with your favorite morning drinks and your favorite memories or conversation!

This recipe is a legacy from my mother-in-law. In fact, as I look through my recipe book I realize that I have at least one favorite dish I associate with most of the people who have been very special in my life.

I've heard of family traditions of passing down specific furniture or jewelry to people. A recipe is so much simpler, and less likely to ignite family battles--except about the rising of yeast!

Maybe I'll pick a few recipes I'd like people to enjoy. I'll imagine being there to share the dish with them. I could include these favorite recipes occasionally in Christmas letters.

This will be the first!

I like to imagine a grandchild of mine baking this traditional bread 30 years from now and telling her or his own stories about the choreg controversy.

BACK TO YOUR OWN SONG OF THE SENSES...

Give yourself some NOW again at three moments of the day today. This time notice and point out to yourself all the sensory details you can define that make up those moment.

Sing Your Song of Senses: Sight Sound Taste Touch Smell

Day 5. THANK THE TENSION AND LET IT GO

Where are you holding tension right this moment?

Is it in your shoulders, your neck, your jaw, your face, your scalp, your buttocks, your torso, your arms, your intestines, your toes? Does your yearning for a massage tell you anything about your need to melt some tension away? Have you ever made a special trip to Nordstroms just to use the foot massage machine?

Ask yourself why your tension is there. Tension is usually the gradual, almost imperceptible tightening of parts of your body over time. You may begin clenching one area in response to cold, nervousness, anger, anxiety, frustration or fear. The clenching serves a purpose in the "flight or fight" response of your body. Clenching draws your body tighter into a more compact unit, easier to defend.

The problem is that you start chronic clenching and forget to let go when your situation changes. Tension becomes your normal pattern. Then when you are under stress, you push the tension even tighter. Or you grind your teeth. The gradual buildup of tension affects breathing, teeth, blood vessels, hair loss, posture, skeleton—it affects all parts of your body.

Tension is often fatal to your sense of humor.

Tension doesn't start out bad. It starts by doing us a favor. So thank the tension in each part of your body and give it some time off. It may feel foolish, but it can increase awareness and build progressive relaxation. Say something like, "OK, neck, thank you for holding that tension and you can let some go now. You can let more go. More. That feels good."

Thank and release tension wherever you find it in your body. Today start with five tension sites. Tomorrow release those same sites again. Gradually you will notice that some of those sites have eased their chronic tension. Move on to one new site to replace each one that improves significantly. Continue this easy awareness until you again use tension only when it is an appropriate response to the situation at the moment.

Thank and release tension wherever you find it in your body.

Day 6. LET EVERY MOMENT BE YOUR MICROCOSM

*Become the change you wish to see
in the world*
Ghandi

The best way to let your life blend business success with personal satisfaction is to let this moment blend success and satisfaction. Bring into this moment the very best and brightest of all the resources at your command. If all the blood surging through your body were suddenly to sing...if all the oxygen in your cells were to play music...if your bones were to paint pictures and your organs were to dance...what would this moment be?

Whom would you include if you could assemble a board of directors from any walk of life, from any moment in time present, past or to come? If you could invite ancestors, role models, people you admire or wonder about to sit in a session and advise you on your life, whom would you gather? What would they talk about. How would they direct you? If all their wisdom and insights and love were guiding you right this moment, how would you be operating?

Today's exercise is to gather such a group in your head. Think of who you want there and what you will talk about.

Here's my own sample guest list from one period in my life:

MY BOARD OF DIRECTORS

Thomas Jefferson - His shining intellect

Lynette - She holds herself lightly in the world

Winnie - Just the thought of her in the family
      gives me a glow

Fred Astair - His fluid grace and spark

Emily Dickinson - The delicacy of her thoughts

Marty - His spirit of the magnificent peasant

Walt Disney - He harnessed his own joy to
      share with others

Grandma Moses - Found her unique primitive
      style in later life

Shari - Breathes reverence into all life's
      moments

Ray Krok - Took his vision into the marketplace
      and exploded in success

I didn't choose them because they are perfect all-round models. Of course they are flawed, they are human! They also represent a range of the practical, the successful, and the playful that I want in all the moments of my life.

If each moment is a microcosm, you have the mental resources to bring into any moment all the blended wisdom of your board of directors to address any challenge or opportunity!

Day 7. FROM EACH MOMENT ACCORDING TO ITS GIFTS...

Don't go to Hawaii for lobster. I was surprised when I visited Hawaii once and noticed a guy order lobster "fresh from Maine" for dinner all three evenings. I wondered why someone would do that. There are so many delicious fish native to the islands. I sampled tuna, ono and mahi-mahi so fresh and flavorful they brought tears of appreciation to my eyes. Why would someone want imported pleasures while passing up the bounty so richly available in front of him?

I never did intrude to find out the diner's reasons for his repetitive selection. Maybe he was on a lobster diet; maybe he made a practice of ordering the most expensive thing on the menu even if he never varied his diet; maybe he was CEO of a lobster distributor and felt he was marketing. He had his reasons. Maybe he just loved lobster.

He did prime my thinking, though. When do I do something similar? When do I think I know best what gifts I should take from each moment? When do I spend so much time controlling that I spend so little time celebrating?

For today, find a treasure that is specific to today. Find some element of the weather, the daily process, the news, your relationships, your health, your spirit that are worth special attention just as they are now.

Inebriate of air am I, and
debauchee of dew...
Emily Dickinson.

Get drunk on too much golden air. Run your fingers through dew-dappled grass. Close your eyes and smell this specific delicious day, unique in all of eternity. Find the nuggets of gifts embedded in the people you see. Find the nuggets in you.

Here are two brief reports on tasting small moments.

HAPPINESS IS KNIT
FROM A VERY THIN THREAD

If ever I find a quarter,
I take it as an invitation
to call someone I love
And tell them
I'm feeling lucky
and thinking of them.

It's an inordinate amount of joy
for 25¢.

And sometimes
I plant a quarter
for someone else to find.

Never knowing what they
will choose to do
with their lucky feeling.

Happiness is knit from a very thin thread.

MY BROTHER GAVE HIMSELF A CONSONANT

Our family is frugal,
maybe even cheap.

Even so,
we are like many people who elect to indulge
in a wild extravagance
to celebrate at least
one milestone birthday
in their lives.

When my brother turned 40
he let us all know.
He wanted a second "N" on his nickname.
From "Cornelius," to "Con" to "Conn".

Was he tired of being associated
with "con games"?
Or did he want to call up images
of Irish warrior kings?

I don't know.
But I give him now the "N."

When I turned 50
I didn't know how I wanted
to mark the date.

Lately it has come to me.

I like the words "low and loose."
I can drop my voice low—
no longer choosing to be high and fluttery

attracting attention
and pleading to be liked.

My bones can go loose—
I don't need to clench my shoulders
or my neck.
I can swing my arms as I walk
And feel the spaces between my bones.

What rich luxuries for a frugal family.

CHAPTER THREE

Shape
The Meaning

THE SIGNIFICANT SHOELACE

Picture yourself getting off an airplane in Orlando, Florida, on the day before Thanksgiving, the busiest travel day of the year, at the start of a family holiday. Not only did the plane land late after a noisy flight with almost no attention from flight attendants, but you are missing a shoelace. You started this trip from JFK airport in New York with a perfectly good pair of new shoes with two shoelaces. Now you are standing in Orlando waiting for your baggage and you have one snug shoe and one floppy foot. Does this sound like a dismal harbinger of vacation aggravations to come?

Not necessarily. Thanksgiving week, 1994, Theresa and Santiago deBara were taking their young daughter, Amanda, to Disneyworld for a holiday treat. TWA flight 265 was packed with 213 passengers. At 30,000 feet cruising altitude, Theresa started to feel pains she thought were false labor since she was only 7 months pregnant. The pains got worse and the deBaras asked flight attendants for help. Theresa stretched her 5-foot-7 frame out across 5 seats as contractions started.

An internist who had delivered only one baby 13 years earlier responded to the request for medical assistance. He ordered an emergency landing at the nearest airport. At 9:40 a.m., still 90 miles from Dulles airport, the baby arrived with the umbilical cord around his neck. He was not breathing and he was rapidly turning blue. Another couple on board were paramedics from Massachusetts. They had delivered about a dozen babies and one of them specialized in infant respiratory procedures.

There were no straws on board to help suction fluid from the baby's lungs. One flight attendant had a juice box with a bendable straw. Though he doubted that the baby would survive, Dr. Rachlin administered CPR while the paramedic used the straw. It worked. They still needed something clean to tie off the umbilical cord. A brand new shoelace.

The shoelace worked too. The baby's breathing stabilized. The plane landed at Dulles. The premature baby, 4 pounds 6 ounces, 17 inches long was in critical but stable condition and improved gradually but steadily. His parents selected for him the first name of "Matthew" meaning "gift from God." Matthew Dulles deBara is called a "miracle baby" by many who witnessed the series of fortunate circumstances that brought him so dramatically into the world.

Now, back to imagining you had landed in Orlando without that shoelace. How would you be feeling?

The very circumstances that tend to annoy, frustrate or anger us can be totally transformed when we infuse them with a different significance or perspective.

Life gets to say what happens. You always get to say what it means.

THE KAYAKER'S CREED

Do you like outdoor recreation? Do you like the fresh air, the beauty, the sense of nature, vitality, expansiveness of being alive and active in the out of doors?

Stephen Daniel is a professor of philosophy at Texas A & M University. A few years ago he became an ardent kayak enthusiast. He loved the vigorous outdoor stimulation, the sense of connection with the water as he was gliding through and keeping a precarious balance in the small, sleek craft.

He and some university friends decided to spend part of the Christmas holiday on a five-day kayaking trip 162 miles down the Durango river canyon in Mexico. The first day out went perfectly—pure air, beautiful canyon scenery, hearty friendships, good food and a full deep night of sleep.

On the second day, Daniels overturned his kayak in some rushing water and it wedged itself between some rocks. He managed to get the kayak upright, but he couldn't break free of the rocks. He sat in that kayak in mountain-melt cold water for almost 24 hours waiting for a rescue helicopter.

He was airlifted to a hospital in Texas where they finally told him that his lower limbs had been so cold for so long that they would have to amputate both legs at the knees. He came through the surgery and went back to teaching. He was interviewed later and he remarked "I'm glad I'm not a roofer because if I worked in construction and couldn't work I wouldn't know who I was."

He noted that as a professor of philosophy he dealt in flexibility and thinking options so he knew he would be fitted with artificial limbs and kayak again, but in the meantime he could also find happiness. "Look at me now, here in this wheelchair. I'm in the position of a permanent kayaker, and life is my river now."

Life gets to say what happens. You always get to say what it means.

INVOLUNTARILY SEPARATED FROM EARNING A PAYCHECK

A close friend was involuntarily separated from earning a paycheck. He wrote this:

"It wasn't too bad when I first got laid off. We'd seen it happen to friends so it wasn't shocking or devastating at the moment. We had a little money saved. In a way it was a relief. Waiting for the ax to fall had been almost worse than the reality.

I gave myself a pause. Really thought about what to do next. What industries would be growing for the next 10-20 years? What could I do that wouldn't consume me like my last position? How could I be at the forefront of something and retire in 10 years? It was scary, but also stimulating.

I made the rounds. Took all my contacts out for long lunches to probe for possibilities. Somehow a year went by. We called it The Year of Living Frugally. We had cut back on everything we possibly could in our household and how we had to think seriously of moving.

A company I'd been advising wanted to hire me part time. My wife's business picked up a little. We're making it O.K. While we have few indulgences, we are celebrating the gifts of what we do have.

*It feels like my career direction was inter-
rupted and it took me the longest time to
accept that the old direction was NOT coming
back. It was hard to let go of what I thought I
had wanted to achieve. It was the death of
certainty.*

*Now I'm grateful and happy. I've been lucky
enough to survive and have the resources to
explore new options for the uncertain future."*

Life gets to say what happens. You always
get to say what it means.

Life
charges
tuition,

like most places
where you can
learn a lot.

THE BEAUTIFUL NEW HOUSE

I noticed a beautiful house on a walk through the neighborhood as I visited a friend in North Carolina. The house was new and welcoming, set perfectly on a flowing lawn in an inviting neighborhood. Lights were on in many windows and two kids and a dog were playing in the yard at twilight near the blooming dogwood trees. I mentioned the warmth of the scene to my friend as I came in from my walk.

"It is a new house ," she commented. *"The couple bought it, moved in, and then his company started downsizing. The story came out later that he was worried that he might be cut. He was driving home from work one day and had a flat tire on the beltway. It was a rainy evening and he started to change the flat. He had the trunk open, the old tire off, the spare out of the trunk and maybe something snapped.*

Maybe he was in despair, maybe he was just cold and wet and hated getting his clothes all smeared. Halfway through changing that flat, he stepped out into the road and met a semi truck at full speed."

Life gets to say what happens. You always get to say what it means.

CLOSER TO HOME

My husband just turned 55. Most of his mid-decade birthdays have been marked by concerns about health and aging. They are usually the occasion for long moody silences, a round of visits to doctors, new resolves about exercise, a dogged review of our bills and finances, curiosity about how to avoid or disguise impending baldness, a series of physical complaints, general grumpiness.

I'm not sure what changed him this year. But these were some of his reactions. He ordered his first "senior special breakfast" at Denny's. He mentioned his birthday to two sets of friends and we all went to dinner. He bought a dining room table—something he has wanted for our entire 21 years together and which we've never had before. He wore a Mickey Mouse tie that his sister got him. He made a Ta-Da list highlighting special events of the last year and basked in remembering them. He joked that "the only thing I have to look forward to is nostalgia."

What has caused this revolution? I don't know. But I'm sure enjoying it now.

Life gets to say what happens. You always get to say what it means.

THE GEEZER EQUINOX
A Father Reflects

What does it mean
to be twice as old as your son?

In my 20,000 days on earth
I've accumulated
(in no particular order)
a set of golf clubs,
one child,
and a series of cars.

I've let go of
both parents,
several companies,
and most of my hair.

My son at 10,000 days old
is working now in Italy
designing telecommunications equipment.
He slipped right into the global economy
while I was out somewhere buying socks.

I still don't know what this means
and it wasn't what I expected.

Today's paper reports that
Marlon Brando is 70 years old
and Barbie doll is 35.

Some days I am so surprised
by the stranger in my mirror.

BERNIE'S QUESTION

Bernie Siegel, author of LOVE, MEDICINE AND MIRACLES, suggests that people experiment with shifting two sentences. "Why me?" And "What will I do with this?"

People who get cancer ask themselves, "Why me?" People who win the lottery ask themselves, "What will I do with this?"

Siegel suggests that you turn those sentences around. When you are touched by good fortune ask yourself "Why me?" Think of what this gift will empower you to do. Think of why you personally might be the channel of this fortune in positive directions.

When you get ill or suffer bad fortune ask yourself, "What will I do with this?" Think of the hidden resources in you or your life that can come into play to work with this new reality. Flex your muscles for shaping your future.

Life gets to say what happens. You always get to say what it means.

A WEEK OF SHAPE THE MEANING

So how do you shape the meaning of what happens to you? Think of the shape of a loaf of bread. One restaurant in Hilton Head, South Carolina, served bread in flower pots. It was an interesting gimmick and didn't change the taste or texture of the bread. It started me realizing, though, that bread assumes the shape of the pan or pot you bake it in.

The dough is your experience, the "stuff" that happens to you in life. You select the pan that gives that experience its shape in the cooker/oven of your mind.

Day 1. LET GO OF ANGER, RESENT-MENT, REGRET

Anger, resentment and regret trap you in the past. The one absolute thing we know about the past is that it is over. In my favorite scene in the Disney movie, THE LION KING, we see Rafiki, the wise mentor, hitting Simba, the lion cub, in the head with a stick.

"Ow. That hurts. Why did you do that?" Complains Simba.

"Doesn't matter, it's in the past." Comments Rafiki. A moment later Rafiki tries to strike again and Simba ducks.

"Now you see, you learn from the past." Rafiki observes.

The past is for learning from. It may send emotional and experience echoes into the present. We can move through them and get on to today. Every hour I spend as a victim of my past is one hour I don't contribute toward today.

On regret. Have you ever noticed that when you are sad about a missed opportunity you almost always imagine the rosiest possible outcome of that opportunity? You rarely just shrug and think that you still get to have that singular experience in the future for the first time.

A friend had an option to publish a book about 4 years ago. She occasionally daydreams wistfully about where her career would be today if that book had been a bestseller and positioned her profitably at the peak of her field.

She never imagines that the book might have created a big yawn in the marketplace and bruised her confidence forever. Or that she might have written too soon before her considerable insights of the past few years.

We often regret the sunny road not taken. And because we did not take it, we never saw that it had potholes and detours too.

For today, let go of one regret, anger or resentment.

Day 2. SAY IT NEW TO SEE IT NEW

Look again at the example from Day 1, my friend who had not published the book 4 years ago. She had been saying to herself "If only." "If only I had published my book back then I'd be famous, wealthy, established, respected, a leader in the field today."

She came up with a better phrase to help her say it new to see it new. She replaced "If only," with "How fortunate." "How fortunate that I got four more years to refine my ideas, that I had time to develop better contacts in the publishing world, that I learned more about the marketplace. How fortunate that I didn't publish too soon."

Saying it new doesn't change any circumstances. It does change your perception of how to make the most of your current reality.

Another friend asked, "How can I get over the dull, drained feeling that my day is too full of obligations, that all my energy goes to doing stuff I have to do?"

One small adjustment is to transform the phrase "got to" to "get to." You don't change the number of things you will do. You honor your choice in the matter. You refuse to be a helpless pawn and exercise freedom to participate in your day. You open your spirit to the possibility that because you are choosing these things you may invite joy into them.

HARD ROLLS IN THE BRONX

When I was about seven years old my folks took us to visit relatives in the Bronx, New York. Auntie lived on the top floor of a five-floor walkup apartment building on Briggs Avenue. Five long flights of stairs, no elevator, lots of luggage.

After the long drive from Indiana, my parents yearned for many remembered big-city treats. First were those crispy hard rolls fresh from the bakery for breakfast every morning. My younger sister and I were sent down five flights to the corner bakery every day for the rolls.

The first day was fun. We dawdled and played the whole way down and back up all those steps. By the second day we were complaining about the climb back up the five flights of steps. I somehow imagined that enough complaining would eliminate the task. They were deaf to our whining.

On the third day we trudged to the bakery, begrudging every step. We even refused to eat one of the magical rolls when we got home. "They just had us kids to send us on errands." I pouted.

On the fourth day I had one of those blinding insights kids can get.

"If we are going to end up going anyway, no matter how much we protest, why not enjoy the trip?" We dawdled down the steps again, inventing games as we twisted ourselves around the wrought iron railing. We got outside and noticed the pulse of the city, the variety of the neighborhood, the exotic mingling of smells from the boot shop, the florist, the tobacconist, and the bakery all in a row.

The bakery itself was a celebration of senses. My nose tickled with a sniff of confectioner's sugar that even smelled sweet (how can I smell a taste?). We hiked the Himalayan steps home and enjoyed the breakfast rolls with the adults. The kitchen glowed with steaming tea, crunchy golden poppy-seed rolls and the laugh-laced conversation and memories of the grown-ups.

Flicking one little brain switch from "got to" to "get to" gave me that scene which is still a gift so many years later.

Today when you look at your list of all the things you've "got to" do, remember that you have choices. These are what you "get to" do if you want to be a spouse, parent, sister, brother, friend, professional, citizen.

You always have a choice.

Day 3. REVISIT COSMIC PERSPECTIVE

I think I'll make a T-shirt that shows the universe spinning and expanding through eternity, and put a small locator arrow on the tiny state of Maryland in the teeny portion near Washington D. C. on the infinitesimal speck of Montgomery County and the atom that is Rockville. The arrow, of course, will say "You Are Here."

It will help remind me that I am a small speck in an enormous universe. You are too.

Yet an ant sees you as gigantic and enormously powerful. Which are you today?

Take a few moments to zoom in and zoom out on your life.

Zooming in. How are you overall as an organism using up air on earth today? How are your bodily systems? Your organs? Are your lungs doing O. K.? Are your cells working away, your platelets floating along? Are there atoms of new fingernails forming right this second? Is your big toe doing exactly what it should? Are your eyelids constantly moisturizing those great eyes? Is your liver doing it's usual effective cleanup job? Are your bones and muscles ready to hold you erect or help you bend whenever you choose? Are your fingers ready to move, to touch, to form, to feel?

Zooming out. Imagine you had a telescope-camera mounted inside your own eyes with infinite viewing capability. You could look out your eyes and see as far as your nose, your fingertips, the wall in front of you, the yard beyond your window, the miles to your horizon, the sky as far as the sun, deep space out to the milky way and beyond, you could see farther than time and light can travel and still there is more.

In a universe from the atom to infinity, where are you? In a universe from the atom to infinity, you are here.

You can do some similar thinking about time. Biologists think of a generation as 20 years. But a single handshake can easily span a generation of 80 years. My uncle Haig who is 90 could easily have shaken hands with an older statesman when he immigrated to this country as a 10-year-old boy.

That older statesman, who would have been in his 80's at the time, could easily have shaken hands as a boy with Abraham Lincoln in the 1850's. A woman who had shaken hands with Lincoln as President could easily have shaken hands with Jefferson as a young woman. And so it goes backwards in time till I realize that only 5 generations of handshakes separate me from William Shakespeare.

Look at your hand for a moment. Think of all the people you have touched in a lifetime. Think of all the people they have touched. Think of how far back all those touches reach across time. And through children and grandchildren, how far they will reach into the future.

Consider both your significance and insignificance. Celebrate your unique position in all of time and in all of the universe.

Uncle Armen Says...

Whenever I play golf
I look down at the grass
and I'm glad
I'm on this side
of it.

Day 4. TAKE THE LIFE BALANCE INVENTORY

How well are you doing in the seven zones of life? Maybe it is a good idea to take a quantifiable look at how you would rate yourself on the **LIFE BALANCE INVENTORY** at the back of this book.

Over 2000 people from the United States, Mexico and Canada have completed this inventory. Most of them report being pleasantly surprised. They find that they are doing fine in most of the zones. They also see at least one area which they'd like to improve. Many people copy the inventory and share it with a friend. They talk over their results and set some goals and help each other reach them. Some people even take the inventory as part of their personal annual review. It can be helpful to see progress or to notice creeping neglect.

Complete the inventory. Talk with someone about what you learned.

Day 5. PLAY WITH COOPERATION AND CONTROL

Do you ever find yourself controlled by your need to control? This has to be one of life's jokes on us. Like realizing that I instantly dislike someone who is judgmental. Wow, that's a quick judgment!

Some of the most tormented people I know are those with the strongest need to control. The torment springs from the reality that there aren't too many things they do control. When I accidentally fall into my own control trap I lose all sight of what is within my control and what is not. I agonize over trying to control something I can't control and neglect what is easily within my realm to control.

I can never hear the Serenity-Courage-Wisdom Prayer too often. " God, grant me the serenity to accept the things I cannot change, the courage to change the things I can, and the wisdom to know the difference."

It is helpful to remember that several amazing things happened in this universe even before I was born. Other amazing things happened during my lifetime that I had nothing to do with. Still more will happen after I've gone to the great reading room with big comfortable couches in the sky. So why should I imagine myself to be in charge?

I do much better when I focus on cooperation. I think about being part of the unfolding of life.

I am one petal, one pebble, one dewdrop, one butterfly. I am here. I bring moisture, beauty, weight, substance to wherever I am. I am affected by the breeze, by the rain, by the sun, by the starlight, by the earthquake, by the rainbow.

This is tough sometimes when I am stuck in traffic. But when I can do it, I stay much more calm, much more grounded in the resources that will improve my day and my life.

Breathing in, I relax; breathing out, I smile.

Today, let go of 3 things you don't control. Make a physical gesture of letting go of them. Let them fly away from you. Feel lighter and more free that they are gone.

The Secet of Tennis:

Life
is like tennis.
It's better
once you know
how to serve.

Day 6. REVEL IN SMALL SANITIES

Small sanities are those celebrations of the senses or the spirit that we can give ourselves on a daily/weekly basis. These are the small refreshers that restore and renew us. Here's a sampling of typical and unusual items from my audiences over the years:

Take a Bubble bath
Visit the zoo
Ride a bike
Bathe by candlelight
Fly a kite
Plant flowers
Bathe the dog and get wet
Play with a toy
Wade in a stream or a fountain
Take someone on a picnic
Wash the car
Visit with a friend
Meditate
Go to church or temple
Listen to music
Buy something new
Cook
Eat
Rest your eyes with a damp cloth or
        slices of cucumber over them
Sleep
Draw
Wear power lingerie
Play cards
Play golf
Play with a kid or dog (borrow one
        if necessary)

Take a walk
Give something away
Dance
Exercise
Have a picture of your family at the office and
     a picture of your office at home
Drink an exotic coffee
Read a book
Take a ride in the country
Garden
Eat fruit
See a movie
Play with clay or dough that you knead
Take a kid for ice cream
Learn something new
Write a letter

Another category of small sanities is
CANDELISM. This is the opposite of
vandalism. In candelism you do something
unexpected and kind for someone else. Pay
the toll for a stranger behind you, leave a
quarter in a phone coin return slot for someone to find, surprise a colleague with a fresh
cup of coffee or tea, leave a love message on
your spouse's voicemail. This is unencum-
bered joy.

Day 7. PICTURE YOUR YEAR

This is the last day of our week to focus on SHAPE THE MEANING. So why not do an exercise with lines, forms and shapes? You can do this through sketches, clip art, computer draw, stick figures, pasting pictures cut from magazines, you can use toothpicks or popsickle sticks. The idea is to move beyond just words and to try to let your ideas take actual shape or form.

Draw a mural of the year you have just had or the one you are about to have. Think back over your Ta-Da list, your challenges, your goals met and your goals that have changed, travel, play, family, health, spirit, community, finance. Place a shape at the center of your page that most reflects how the year has been overall. Some examples might be a star, heart, box, sun, diamond, circle, face, trophy, arrow up or down. Inside that shape, put the numerals for the year and a word or phrase that best crystallizes the year.

Around the page, sketch some icons or symbols of major events or accomplishments. Include three to ten. Mix words with the symbols. If you are still wondering what else to include, here are a few more options:

- Something you learned
- An interesting person you met
- An opportunity
- A setback
- Something surprising
- Vacation

- A sense of accomplishment
- Something worth striving for
- A great day
- Something funny
- A treasured moment

A mural like this is interesting to do on the year gone by. It is also valuable to do on January 1 to plan for the year ahead. Instead of New Year's Resolutions that leave you feeling guilty, why not design the coming year with a festive heart? My family and I each do our own and then gather to share them. It's a wonderful way to share some plans and dreams and see if we can help each other reach them.

Forget New Year's Resolutions and create a mural of the year to come.

AFTER INTENSE INPUT

I once went to two conferences almost back-to-back. Each was excellent. Something about conferences, though, is too rich for me.

After the first one I resolved that too much noise prevents me from hearing. Except for life-threatening emergencies, if it needs to be shouted, I probably don't need to hear it.

After the second rich conference I asked myself, "What would you have preferred?"

The answer came to me as a whimsical over-stated fantasy. Just thinking of it helped me go back and shape the meaning and enjoy the juices of each experience. Here's the answer my playful mind gave me.

AFTER THE CONFERENCE

The First Annual Conference on Quiet caused quite an uproar.

The organizers seemed to have thought of everything.
They had selected a perfect location,
    a quiet hideaway
      far from airport and traffic noise
      caressed by gentle sounds of nature.
      They had even tranquilized the louder
          birds.

The program ranged from the predictable to
the practical.
> From "The Sounds of Silence,"
> To "Solitude and the Spirit,"
> From "High-Impact Silence for Public
> > Speakers,"
> To "The Darker Side of Silence,"
> > which dealt with that moment
> > when you knew you were being
> > fired but the words hadn't yet
> > been spoken.

They had even brought in signers
Who could use the hieroglyphics of hands
To translate for those deaf to the language
> of silence.

Sessions were scheduled for first light and
> twilight
To catch the quietest crests of the day.

Meeting rooms were renamed after the
> chambers of the heart.
Eminent faculty were brought in from
> around the globe
To accent the international flavor of silences.
All presenters were coached in never uttering
> a syllable.

Mashed potatoes and gravy were served at
> every meal.
The dress code specifically forbade taffeta and
> noisy jewelry.

And in the final uproar
They discovered
That silence itself was a subtle aphrodisiac.

When one pair
found a passion beyond peace,
Piercing the still night air
with lustful screams
that finally faded into

silence.

CHAPTER FOUR

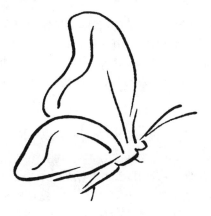

Hold
The Mission

THE TRUCKER ON THE CALL-IN SHOW

I was on a call-in talk show once in Raleigh, North Carolina. The host interviewed me about my second book and we started taking calls. I'd been talking about how helpful it is to define your life mission. I recommended that listeners take a tip from organizations, and define their mission.

The mission statement is a clear and concise summary of what your life is for. Such a statement can help simplify and guide a wide range of choices in both business and personal life.

The next caller said, "I'm a truck driver. Somehow the idea of a mission statement is too fancy for me. What can you suggest that's a little more down to earth?" We joked a moment and I finally asked him "If you can't give yourself a mission statement, could you at least give yourself a bumper sticker?"

He agreed that maybe he could do that. We finished the show with other callers and I went away with that echo in my head. Maybe this stuff is too fancy. Maybe it's the mental plaything of someone like me, lucky enough to have time to think about abstract ideas like my mission on earth. Maybe I was out here telling people nice stuff that can provide toys for the mind on a rainy afternoon. Maybe I'm providing nothing more substantial than whipped cream on the baked potato of life. It bothered me.

At 4 a.m. the next morning I came fully awake. I remembered that my brief 10-word mission statement had kept me aloft during two tough years. I was failing to credit my mission statement for that support. I was taking for granted the subtle contribution my mission statement makes in my life.

My simple statement had helped me through a business downturn, economic losses, the theft of my jewelry, including my treasured wedding ring, the final transfer of my Mom with Alzheimer's disease into the nursing home, and numerous other setbacks that were less traumatic. Why was I doubting its impact? I dozed again about 6 a.m. and woke later, fresh in the joy, clarity and simplicity that come from knowing my purpose.

As a kid I had learned from catechism that my purpose in life was to know, love and serve God in this life and be happy with him in heaven. Somehow I had drifted from this simplicity and wanted something else. Something that honored all the resources I had been blessed with and applied them to the process of being on earth. Something that celebrated my uniqueness and suggested how that uniqueness might contribute to my world.

It doesn't matter whether you call it a bumper sticker or a mission statement. It doesn't matter whether it is in words or images. It only matters that you select the ideas, words or images and hold them clearly in your life to guide and smooth daily decisions and directions.

At the corporate level that is exactly what saved Johnson and Johnson during the Tylenol tampering. They went back to their mission statement and recognized instantly that the only priority was the absolute safety of their customers. They pulled all their stock from store shelves and left a lasting impression on the public by living their mission so thoroughly.

Sometimes we are like companies which try to create comprehensive mission statements packing in so much that essence is obscured. This happens when a task force goes off for a week-long retreat to "hammer out" a mission statement. They come back and distribute a lofty pronouncement of purpose. Everyone in the company gets a copy on beautiful vellum paper to post prominently. Ask someone a week later what the mission is and they will reply, "It's over there in a drawer somewhere."

Here's a clue. If it's "over there in a drawer somewhere," it ain't your mission statement. Maybe it is better to think of it as a bumper sticker. Something short, a distillation of your essence, something you have with you all the time, something you keep on your bumper to help cushion life's collisions.

GETTING TO ESSENCE: THE SMALLEST HINT OF ANTLER

Here's a provocative question. Why ARE you on earth? You don't have to think about this every day before you even brush your teeth. But if you never think about it at all, you spin or churn through life as nothing more than a good WalMart customer and a Redskins fan.

Why are you on earth? Answering this question is like looking for a deer in the woods. Harvey's grandfather says that you won't spot a deer by looking for the whole thing. "Don't look for a big brown creature," he said. "Look for the smallest hint of antler, a tiny glimpse of white tail, listen for the rustle—and for the stillness."

You won't usually define your mission all at once. It may come to you over time. In the dark. In the quiet. As you swim or cook. As you watch a child sleep or see a partner learn new software. There are some exercises you can do to invite it to come closer to you.

When it comes all the way home it will feel so comfortable it may be a disappointment. But it will fit and you will find the peace of having something that fits just right.

A friend once confessed, "I finally figured out what God wants me to be and I hate it. He wants me to be ordinary."

HOLD THE MISSION - The Focus of Week 3

An image for this principle is a full, juicy apple. The apple in kids' books went with the letter "A," the most basic building block of the alphabet. The apple symbolizes getting the real basics of life. And it is sweet, nourishing, and carries the seeds of its own future. Not a bad symbol.

Here are some exercises to help you come up with your own mission statement or bumper sticker. The more clearly you can define your mission, the more it supports your decisions and directions.

Day 1. SKETCH A LOGO

*Trust your hunches. They're usually
based on facts filed away
just below the conscious level.*
Joyce Brothers

Corporations often use a logo to establish a unified and unique identity in the marketplace. The best logos are simple, but the creation and selection of the right logo employs a lot of creativity and resources. Corporations know that their logo is an enormously powerful tool for both their external customers and their internal customers.

Participants in one of my seminars have come up with great logos for themselves.

One man calls himself Mr. B+. He explained: "B+ reminds me to always Be Positive. It is also my blood type, and I give blood every 56 days. I'm young and busy in my career now, but that is one way I can do a community service every two months."

Another guy came up with a logo of the number "1" atop a dash with the letter "M" beneath the dash. "I use it to remind myself that I am one in a million. Nobody else is like me so I have to do what I have to do because nobody else can do it. I also don't have to get upset with others when we disagree because they are themselves and not me."

One woman drew a joyful stick figure of an aerobic dancer. Life for her involves getting in there, getting active, getting sweaty, getting healthy, getting in shape, and loving it all.

Sit there with pen and pencil and paper. Let your mind drift. Come up with a few images. Sketch them without asking what they mean. Play.

When you talk to yourself... don't interrupt!

Day 2. ASK YOURSELF SOME GREAT QUESTIONS

Kind words can be short and easy to speak,
but their echoes are truly endless.
Mother Theresa

When is the last time you talked to yourself and didn't start out with, "Listen, jerk."

This is a good time for a "getting to know you," conversation with yourself. I've had executive speech coaching clients who took the questions below and answered some of them into a microcassette tape recorder as they waited for an airplane. Or they wrote out answers which we talked over later. Or they talked out loud to themselves and told me some of their reactions. Others talked the questions over with a spouse, friend or colleague. The format isn't important. The visit with yourself is.

Here are some questions to consider. Spend about 20 minutes on this exercise. Answer the ones that appeal to you and ignore the rest.

What was your first job and what did you learn from it?
What's your earliest family memory, school memory, work memory, spouse/friend memory?
What gives you a strong sense of satisfaction in work? Outside work?
Are you more attached to the process of what

you do or the results you create?

Is your life more of a comedy, drama, fantasy, romance, science fiction or horror movie?

One moment in your life that gave you strong insight...

Something you have always been good at...

Something you've always wanted to learn...

Something you love so much you could teach it to others...

Something you feel very strongly about...

If you had 1 year of unlimited resources and no responsibilities you would...

The things you laugh at most...

Recurring themes in your life...

People compliment you on your...

You're attracted to work that...

You're attracted to people who...

Something you wish you had invented...

What do you think about when you wake up in the middle of the night?

What is one dream that has come true in your life?

What's the best holiday or vacation you've ever had?

What is your most treasured possession?

If you were a tree/animal, what kind would you be?

What is one thing in your life that you would choose to do differently if you could choose again?

The place you feel most at home...

The time you feel most satisfied...

How would the person you want to be spend this very day?

If your skills and talents could be put to their highest and best use you would...

Day 3. WRITE YOUR BUMPER STICKER

Think again about all the answers to the questions above. Quiet time is valuable here. Look especially for recurring themes of success and satisfaction.

Draft a mission statement or bumper sticker. Experiment, plunge in, write 3 or 10. Jump in, make mistakes. Try on several to see what fits. Try again. Don't rush. Let the process be organic and natural. Pare it down to 25 words or less.

Here are some samples.
- To succeed in a competitive world and win respect and recognition for myself and others like me.
- To live each day in the joyful appreciation of the gift of life itself.
- To make a difference in the world through my technical skills and to live life to the fullest in both work and play.
- To be the magnificent peasant, respecting survival and appreciating simple pleasures every day.
- To open minds about what is good and important and to keep my own mind constantly stimulated.
- To glow with life and learning, inviting others along.

Start with a phrase like:
- To nourish,
- To triumph,
- To thrive,

- To glory,
- To explore,
- To laugh,
- To revel,
- To invite,
- To cooperate,
- To embrace,
- To be...

Caution: Choose language that invites you to energy and opens your opportunities rather than burdens you with obligations.
Avoid...
- To struggle,
- To survive,
- To battle,
- To terminate.

One colleague wrote a 2-page mission satement and just couldn't cut any further. She finally read it to a few people and asked them what stood out as they listened. She collected their phrases and wove them into a simpler statement.

If your mission statement is as long as *WAR and PEACE*, how can you turn it into a tattoo?

Day 4. REVISIT YOUR GIFTS FROM THE DARK

The older I get the more I notice that some of life's greatest gifts have come to me in my darkest moments. Think back over some of your dark times. What gifts did they bring you? How have they been pivotal in guiding your life?

Each traumatic loss or transition feels entirely unique. Loss of innocence, death of someone close, loss of a job, children moving away, loss of a relationship, loss of youth. The pain can be so sharp and bitter that you hug your solitude and hope to heal. And yet, after many losses, you notice some patterns. You notice what losses can add to your life.

1. DEPTH Times of loss are times that you feel most deeply. You have a new recognition of sacredness and significance in your life. You will only ever feel happiness to the extent you are capable of feeling sorrow. Maybe it is from your deepest pain, anger, despair that you form and flex your power. This power later helps you transform those difficult emotions into your foundation for joy.

2. CLARITY The second gift is clarity. This is a time when you know suddenly what is important and what is just window dressing in your life. This is a time when you know for sure that any problem you can solve with money is more of an inconvenience, not a catastrophe. This is when you reevaluate what is important and what is critical in your life. It is usually a time when love, health and soul leap to the top of the list instantly.

3. CONNECTION You are often surprised by support and comfort from unexpected sources. There is no feeling you will ever feel that others haven't felt before and lived through. You know again that you are part of a bigger human family. You know that you can also touch other people and help them bear their pain.

4. EMPATHY Every person you ever encounter goes through these same losses. Loss doesn't always show up externally. So the person behind the checkout counter at the store, or the person whose driving is bothering you, or the person giving you a hard time about an invoice—any of them might be in the early days of recovery from a major loss. It's not a bad idea to live gently in the world.

5. JOY A major loss helps you refresh your perspective on the daily riches you can easily overlook in your hurry through your stuffed schedule. Suddenly a sunny morning is some-thing to savor. A child's laugh is a treasure to store in your heart. A simple daffodil reflects all the spirit of springtime. A loving touch takes on all the meaning of your marriage vows. You rediscover abundant joy.

After my Mother died, grief came to me as troubled thoughts of those last years while she was ill. I had replaced my image of a younger, healthier Mom with the Mom I was with in the nursing home. I had forgotten her laughing vigor in the fullness of her life.

One day, about ten months after her death, I was standing in a hotel lobby and a stranger, way across an open courtyard, sneezed. It was a wonderful robust sneeze, so loud I could hear it across 50 paces.

Suddenly I revisited my mother in all her youthful glory. I had forgotten her magnificent sneeze, as full and loud as her laugh. She came home to me on the wings of a sneeze.

REMEMBRANCE OF MOM

My mother had a sneeze
that could flatten a Sumo wrestler.

It started down at her toenails
and gathered force on its ascent
toward the mouth of the volcano.
The sound escalated a musical scale,
and her mouth grew wider
with each ascending tone.
Ah...ah...ah...chooo.

She gave herself over to a sneeze,
fully, robustly, completely,
with total commitment.

Yes, she would always turn away politely
to protect others from the explosion of germs.
But once she was seized by a sneeze,
bystanders were at risk.

My own sneeze is too delicate.
Did I fail to get the Sumo sneeze gene
from my mom?

Or was sneezing a skill she secretly cultivated,
a rare mark of abandon
In a pleasantly proper, pedestrian, Indiana life?

Maybe now I'll take up sneezing as a sport
so that every time I sneeze
it will be a tribute to my mom
and a threat to Sumo wrestlers everywhere.

Life Is More Than Your To-Do List

Today, look back at one of the dark times in your life, and one gift you brought from that time into your life today.

There is no path
so dark,
nor road so steep,
nor hill so slippery
that other people have
not been there
before me
and survived.

May my dark times
teach me to help
the people I love
on similar journeys.

Day 5. SELECT A WRITER/PRODUCER FOR THE REST OF YOUR LIFE

If God is your copilot, trade seats!
Sign outside Salem Methodist Church

Ray Bradbury, author of FARENHEIT 451 and many other books, was approached once by film director, Sam Peckinpah. Noted for the violent realism in his work, Peckinpah wanted to film Bradbury's novel SOMETHING WICKED THIS WAY COMES.

"How will you do it, Sam?" Bradbury asked.

"Tear the pages out of your book and stuff them in the camera." Replied Peckinpah.

This conversation between Bradbury and Pechinpah reminds us of a simple truth. Each writer has a distinctive style, each director has a distinctive style.

You are the primary writer and director of your own life story. But suppose you could commission someone to invent the rest of your story? Who would you pick and why?

How would Ernest Hemingway tell the story of your life? How would Jerry Seinfeld? Fannie Flagg? Michael Crichton? Harriet Beecher Stowe? Jackie Collins?

How would Kevin Costner direct it? How would Martha Stewart do it? Clint Eastwood? Milos Forman? Barry Levinson? Mel Gibson?

Penny Marshall? Walt Disney? Barbara Streisand? Bill Cosby? Robin Williams?

Where will your story take place? Who are the main characters? What is the dramatic challenge? Where is the comic relief? Are there any chase scenes? What stars will play the characters?

Which academy award will your story win? For today, play mental badminton with your life story as a book or movie.

Play mental badminton with your life story as a book or movie.

Day 6 DESCRIBE YOUR LEGACY
How do you want to be introduced to God?
Bernie Siegel

It's a bright, sunny afternoon on the day you turn 100 years old. A select group of about 50 people is gathered to salute you and celebrate your centennial. They come with comments honoring your many contributions. Speakers include your relatives, grandchildren, colleagues, mentees, neighbors and friends.

What will you most enjoy hearing from them? What will be the accomplishments or contributions with which you are most satisfied? What is the lasting legacy you are most pleased to have contributed?

What artifacts from your past will be on display that day that will mean the most to you?
- A photo of your elementary school classmates and teacher?
- Your high school sports trophy?
- The poster from the contest you won?
- Your college transcript?
- A picture with your folks at graduation?
- A letter sweater?
- Cards and letters from friends?
- A favorite book?
- A reference letter from your college advisor that helped you get your first job?
- The license plate from your first car?
- A project you assisted on while new in your career?

- Something you designed or invented?
- Photos of your best friends along the way?
- The annual report from your first year as a partner?
- A copy of the deed to your first home?
- Your wedding photo?
- Birth certificates for your kids?
- The recipe for your mom's apple cake?
- An old box from your dad's cigars?
- A gift from someone whose career you helped?
- Something you wrote or painted?
- Flags from the countries you worked in when the company went global?
- A flower from your garden?
- Five headlines applauding projects that you helped bring to reality?
- A scrawled "thank you" note from school kids you spoke to about careers?

What is one thing you can do today to contribute to that lifetime legacy?

Day 7 CREATE YOUR PERSONAL CREST

As I stumble across the years of my life
trying to recall what it was about,
I find that nothing is really clear.
Marlon Brando

This quote is the first sentence of BRANDO: SONGS MY MOTHER TAUGHT ME, the autobiography Marlon Brando published at age 70. I collect first sentences. I love to see how well a writer invites me into a book in those first few words. I like the tone of humility in this sentence, but I also like it when a writer shows a little more confidence in the story he is about to tell.

A family crest is like a coat of arms. It is a visual representation of what a person, a family, a genetic line stands for. It's a traditional symbolic form of providing the kind of focus and unity that Brando seems to miss.

The gift you are given at your 100th birthday party is that your favorite artist is going to design a personal crest for you and your family. This crest will portray 5-10 icons that symbolize ideas or events of great meaning to you, or themes or elements that have shone through your whole life Your crest might have a slogan with the images.

You create the rough draft for the artist to work from. Sketch the shape for your crest. Add the icons. What colors will the artist use?

Should your crest be done in oils, pastels, watercolors? Should it be cast in gold, silver, bronze, clay? Should it be woven into cloth, made into a quilt, knitted into scarves, hand painted on ties, or erected on a billboard? Should it be engraved in stone or should it be made with match sticks or macaroni on a paper plate? Where will your crest be displayed? Should your crest have a sound? Will it be a home page that comes up every time anyone in the world logs onto a computer?

Other than honoring you, what will your crest do? Whom should it inspire? What message will it convey to those who see it? What would you want it to say to your descendents, to others in your field of work, to people everywhere? If your crest were the only image seen by observers from another galaxy, what would they know about humans?

If music were written about your life would it be a symphony, a ballad, rock & roll, blues, rap, heavy metal, or countrywestern?

Here's the classic formula:
- You were born.
- You did stuff.
- You made a difference
- You left a legacy.

Today, sketch your crest or play with your song to express that bare formula in your unique way.

CHAPTER FIVE

Streamline
Your Structure

THE SOUND OF THE LAST BALL DROPPING...

You just got a phone call. You've been invited to come on a special project with the most illustrious leaders in your field to do some exciting research in a wonderful location. Most basic expenses will be covered and the rewards of this project can help make your next 20 or 30 years more productive, more profitable, more successful and more satisfying. You need to accept the following conditions. You must agree to:

Leave behind all current responsibilities for four weeks.
Delegate all work and home management to someone else.
Focus totally on the project while you are gone.
Call work no more than once a week (20 minutes maximum).
Call home no more than twice a week (20 minutes maximum each).
Apply your very best undistracted resources to the project.
Cooperate with a select team of colleagues on the project.

A friend of mine gave herself just such a phone call. She decided that she was strained to the limit in operating her business and family. She and her doctor saw several choices. If she kept operating at full tilt, she would give herself a heart attack. If she stopped voluntarily and took a 30-day rehabilitation she could change some of the madness in her life.

She resisted mightily the idea that she could take a voluntary medical break. Who would take over, how would anything get done right, when was a time she could go that didn't interfere with budget, taxes, annual report, family vacation, a partner's wedding or Christmas holidays?

Finally she accepted reality. If she didn't take this break voluntarily, her physical systems would pick their own time. There is no right time for a breakdown or a heart attack.

She had to delegate all the balls she ordinarily juggled every day. She had to cover business meetings, customers, association work, marketing activities, family care, household maintenance, pet service, community volunteer work. The ones she couldn't delegate, she had to let fall.

I talked to her the day before she checked into the residential care center. "You have no idea, Maggie, what the sound is of the last ball dropping."

She went away to work on the special project—herself. The illustrious team of colleagues were specialists there to support her. Her time was for reflecting, play, meditation, prayer, swimming, reading, talking, therapy and exercise. Yes, her business lost some opportunities. Yes, she spent much of her own money above what insurance covered. Yes, some people saw her as "weak" or "flawed" for such a public display of vulnerability.

And she came back healthier, stronger, more balanced, more focused, more playful and more productive. One of her first actions on returning was to look at her schedule and eliminate about 20% of the "activities" and "responsibilities," that had crept into her life gradually without her conscious choice.

Imagine the whole new perspective you might have about your own calendar, your schedule, your To-Do list, your bumper sticker, your life after such an experience.

Ask yourself now. How can you more consciously evaluate each item on your schedule in terms of ROR, Return on Resources? Where are you investing time, love, concern, attention that you are not getting back a fair return on that investment?

What are three items in your schedule you can cut without reducing the quality of your life? What are three items on which you can focus with greater awareness to enrich the quality of your life?

GIVE WHAT YOU WANT TO GET

This may be the most elusive idea for stream-lining your structure. And it works. Radiate love and you'll attract love. Radiate joy and you'll attract joy. Radiate prosperity and you'll attract prosperity. Radiate satisfaction and you'll attract satisfaction. If you are lucky, you see the truth of this in love relationships. It is also true for career and security issues. Patch Adams is a dramatic example.

Dr. Patch Adams is a humorist physician. He practices medicine and mirth side by side. He accepts money, vegetables and livestock as fees and treats some patients for free. His entire life is imbued with healing humor.

He lives by a simple belief. If he gives gener-ously each day from all of his skills and talents, he will never go hungry. His retirement plan is the number of people he has helped. He knows there will always be a place for him among the people whose lives he has touched.

He practices healing humor. He sometimes does hospital rounds dressed as an angel. People in recovery love it, even though an occasional patient reports thinking he had died and gone to heaven.

Can social security and IRA retirement plans promise more security or a fuller life? Con-trast Adams approach with the self-focused confusion, concern or anguish many people endure seeking the best path to a dignified old age.

I don't mention Patch Adams so that you will do what he does. I mention him because he can show you what is it like to give fully what you want to get; what it is like to trust so totally that you commit all your resources to one path. He shows what it is like to step out in trust.

What is one gift you have from which you could live more fully? What have you ever done, thought of or dreamed of that could bring your gift more fully into the waiting world?

Where could you eliminate some doubt or ambivalence in your life so that what you give is not sabotaged by your insecurities? How can you trust more fully?

Life Is More Than Your To-Do List

A WEEK OF STREAMLINING STRUCTURE

Day 1. APPLY THE 411 FORMULA

Maybe you absolutely can't go away for a month. Maybe you can. Maybe that's a question to ask yourself seriously. Maybe you don't need a month. Maybe you can borrow a friend's fishing cabin out of season for a week of solitude, or a week of companionship with someone you want to know better. Maybe you can house-sit for someone at work or at church while they go away on business or holiday.

Nutritionists have long studied the Minimum Daily Requirement (MDR) for most vitamins and minerals. What is your MDR of solitude? Do you know how much quiet you need? Do you know how much time you need for reflection, repair or renewal?

Investment counselors have long advised that you should "pay yourself first." They recommend that you set aside some money out of every paycheck that goes toward savings. This money comes out of your check before any other bills are paid. I'm suggesting that you "Pay yourself first" with your schedule too.

Try a 411 experiment. 411 is the general information telephone number. This 411 formula may help you give yourself the information you need in your life.

Give yourself a gift of:
    4 hours a month
        (spread out or all together)
    1 day a quarter
    1 weekend a year

You deserve this time. You need this time. Put yourself high enough on your priority list that you schedule this time. It may cost you more in the long run if you scrimp on this time.

This is your time to do as you please. This is your private time. You are free of responsibility and free of guilt for whatever you choose. Give yourself a fling allowance to spend frivolously. You might go roller skating, get a massage, spend a day alone in a hotel, read a book, drive in the country. You might sleep, eat a hotfudge sundae, soak your feet, lunch at an elegant restaurant, visit an art gallery or play golf. Tap a passion, step out of the ordinary, treat yourself.

The important thing is to make a date with yourself, and keep it.

Maybe applying the 411 formula will even protect you from ever having to call 911 for an emergency.

Right now, today, make an appointment for your 4 hours this month.

Day 2. CLEAR THE GRAVEYARD OF CHOICES PAST

Is there a door in you life you hesitate to open? Most people have at least one such door. This is not a deep psychological test. For most people the answer is simple. It's the door to your closet or garage or basement or attic. The reason you don't like to open it is that you come face to face with stuff collected over time. You are facing the graveyard of choices past.

Looking at the contents of that closet, you are haunted by a thought. At one moment in time you let each of these items into your life. You gave them precious square footage in the tiny slice of earth you occupy.

Usually you are prompted to clear out some space in response to promptings:
- A charity is coming through the neighbor hood and will pick up donations.
- Someone is coming to visit and you need the space in the guest closet.
- You are doing your annual cleanout.
- A neighbor is having a yard sale and invites you to join in.

The process is usually that you look over what is in the closet, garage, attic and find a few things to get rid of.

There is another approach. EMPTY the entire area and find a few things to keep. Screen everything in a first round according to three choices:

KEEP
QUESTION
RECYCLE

The only problems will be in the second group. Go through one more time with the same three questions and whatever falls into the second group this time goes into containers marked RECYCLE with a date one year away. If you haven't wanted or needed it in a year, do you want or need it at all?

Today, select one closet or area you will work on and schedule a date to start. Maybe a first step is to collect clean boxes for storage or to find the phone number for your collection charity. Take a small step. Now.

Day 3. CUT CLUTTER
Clutter is postponed decisions.
Barbara Hemphill

Survey all the areas where you live and work. Make a list of 10 areas that--if cleared or organized--will better support your life. Look in your medicine cabinet, silverware drawer, bill file, appliance manual file, tax records, warranty file, photo albums, address book, seasonal decorations, client file, resume, vacation ideas file, birthday list, videotapes, CD's (music and investments), financial records, credit card file, coupons, car records, most frequently called 800 numbers, college transcripts, will and financial records, even your sock drawer.

Create a hit list of the top 10 you will work on. Finish 10 and write a new list.

Go back over family momentos. Create time capsules for each decade and consider throwing away anything that doesn't fit into your time capsue.

If you've been at your current residence for more than four years, pretend you are moving and get rid of everything you wouldn't take along on a crosscountry move.

Make a kit for tasks that repeat--changing the oil, wrapping gifts, paying bills.

Day 4. CONSOLIDATE YOUR NUMBERS

Even today, my nephew still answers the phone number that my family had when I was a child. That was the only number we had or needed then. And we have held it for 50 years. What a time of innocence.

Today I have more numbers than I can remember. Yes, I keep an alphabetical list of everything, and I also keep a functional list with related numbers grouped together.

Make a consolidated list of your most frequently used numbers and those you need to access in an emergency. Creating this list has two benefits. First, you will have a handy list. Second, you will respect yourself more by noticing that you survive well in an increasingly complex world.

LIST:
- All addresses home, office, cabin
- All phone numbers home, office, cabin, car, beeper, FAX
- All phone numbers for spouse and children
- Child care/Eldercare numbers
- Emergency numbers for fire, police, ambulance, doctor, neighbors
- All techno-numbers; CompuServe, America OnLine, e-mail
- Social security number
- Social security numbers of spouse and children
- Tax ID number
- Driver's license

- Car make, model, serial number and license number
- All airline club frequent traveler numbers
- All hotel frequent traveler numbers
- All car rental credit card numbers
- All credit cards: comprehensive, retail, telephone, gasoline, travel
- Health insurance information
- Model and serial numbers of your computers, printers, FAX and other equipment
- Your height, weight and sizes
- Height, weight and sizes of people for whom you might buy clothes or shoes
- Membership number in health clubs and professional associations
- Checking account number
- Savings account number
- Cleaning service
- Veterinarian, kennel
- Service station
- Hairdresser/barber

Look over the telephone directories of groups you belong to. Use a highlighter pen to mark the numbers you call most often. This helps go right to the needed information when you turn to that page.

Day 5. PRACTICE THE 24-HOUR RULE
Today as you sort through the mail, notice your reactions and try the 24-hour rule.

You probably react happily to any envelope you think contains a personal letter or a check. Those go into the "Open me first," stack, along with anything else that looks like business and requires timely attention (like bills.)

Today's mail will also contain items that are easy to throw away immediately. These usually include advertisements and promo material for things you are not interested in.

It's the third group of items that gets you in trouble. You might be interested in looking at this item or this offer later, but it is not clear or urgent enough to act on immediately. So you put these items into a stack for getting around to later. Each day that stack grows until it takes over your desk, your counter, your "stuffit" drawer, or your entire office.

Why put yourself through that aggravation? As you process today's mail look at each item in group three and ask yourself, "Am I willing to take action on this in the next 24 hours?" If the answer is "No," toss it. Cold, calculating, callous and efficient.

You do not have to be willing to order something or sign up within 24 hours; you just commit to finding the time to read the offer more carefully. If you don't have time for that in this day, chances are you were going to bury it anyway.

Day 6 CUT THE CORD ON TELESELLERS

I pay for my telephone for my own convenience. Telesellers use something I am paying for to inconvenience me.
Jan Zeanah

You do not have to be nice to people who invade your home, your phone line, and your dinner hour to meet their needs to sell. It is perfectly all right to be polite and firm and say "Sorry, I'm not interested."

Some people are too nice to cut off a teleseller. Why is it kinder to listen to them if you will end up saying "No," anyway? Save them and yourself valuable time by an early disconnect.

Yes, the hardest people to say "No" to are charities. If it bothers me to turn down a particular charity, I ask the caller whether he or she is being paid for calling. If I am talking to someone who cares enough about the cause to make the calls as a volunteer, I am tempted to contribute. If I am talking to a paid or commissioned fundraiser I ask myself, "Will my donation go to pay more fundraisers to call more people at dinnertime to raise more money to hire more fundraisers?" Then I ask them to contribute to a scholarship fund I support.

Charities deserve your support. Telefunding is not the only form of support you can offer.

Day 7 MAKE FRIENDS WITH "NO"

Every time you say "No," to any request for time, money, energy, support, you are saying "Yes," to something else. Maybe you are saying "Yes," to spending more time with your family, to using the money to support the charity you have specifically chosen, to having more time for yourself. Behind every "No," is a "Yes."

Revisit your bumper sticker to find the roots of the resounding "Yes!" in your life. Once you hear that "Yes," clearly enough, "No," will be your friend.

Also let go of unrealistic expectations that there is some easy solution out there like flextime or working at home. You'll still have tough choices.

LET'S STOP LYING ABOUT HOME-BASED BUSINESSES

I have been a homebased business for 15 years. After all that time I no longer feel like a homebased business. I know I should be in a new category on the census. I have become an office-based dweller.

The business started out small. One telephone, one computer, one desk, one file. It all tucked neatly into a closet. Eventually it crept into other parts of the house. I fed it a room; it demanded a room and a media closet. I fed it the closet; it demanded space in the garage. I fed it some garage space; it demanded a dedicated FAX line. I fed it a FAX line....

The worst part are the tendrils that talk. The business sends out tendrils of guilt or opportunity every second. The tendrils curl around my ankles and tug at me every time I move anywhere in the house. I head for the kitchen to baste the Sunday dinner and the tendrils whisper, "You could address that envelope as you walk past my door...." "If you just made that one phone call, everything would be easier tomorrow...."

There is hardly ever a time when some part of me isn't hearing that whisper, "What could or should you be doing right now to be more responsive to clients or more profitable for yourself or your investors?"

Yes, I love the short commute. I love the access to files whenever I want them. I love the freedom and flexibility. It's exactly what I want, most of the time.

And sometimes I yearn for a door I can finally close. Sometimes I dream of taking some total time off.

It is easier to say "No" once you make friends with your resounding "Yes!"

A "N-O-L-O-W" DAY

Marty and I took our walk one morning and surveyed the landscape of the day which lay before us. It was a day off without one single scheduled obligation, with 28 hours before either of us had any commitments.

"There's so much we could get done today," he said.
"Where should we begin?" I offered.
"What was that line from Beverly's Grandma McKee?" he asked
"'There's a lot of things on my list today, and one of them is napping. I think I'll start there'." I quoted.
"What if we have a day with no work, a day when we rest, relax and recharge?"

From that inspired idea was born the "N-O-L-O-W" day. Not-One-Lick-Of-Work. It took discipline just to get through that one day without fluttering into one task or another. We went to breakfast, took a nap, walked again, read, ate, watched TV, visited with each other, exercised and slept soundly.

That day taught us something about relaxing. It taught us that we had forgotten how. We had gotten into the habit of hurry, the habit of tasking, the habit of To-Do.

We don't have these days very often, but we welcome them and invite them into our lives.

COMPANIONS AND CONNECTIONS

Life today is increasingly complex. You are stronger and more resiliant amid such complexity if you have an array of companions and connections.

Have you ever made a list of all the roles you need someone for? What if you listed just the top 20?

How many of these roles are filled in your life? You may have the same person, group or pet fill several roles. The big question is: Are the roles that are most important to you all covered in some way? If you have a gaping vacancy, can you fill it by looking for someone with a similar need and helping each other?

- An intellectual challenger - someone with whom to juggle ideas and thoughts
- A comforter - someone to share toast and tea and kindly conversation
- A spiritual companion - someone to share thoughts and silences, depth and reverence
- A kick-you-in-the-keister friend - someone to tell you when you have spinach between your teeth
- A buddy/playmate - someone who calls up the child in you for fresh fun
- A fireside/mellowness friend - someone who feels equally lucky in life
- A rowdy romper - someone with whom to explore physical adventure
- A neighbor - someone to invite to spontaneous Sunday supper or walk

over to visit in the snow
- A shoulder to lean on - someone who can offer comfort and maybe guidance
- A role model (accepting human imperfections) - someone who does anything at a level to which you aspire
- A joy buzzer - someone who reminds you of your abundant humanity
- An awe companion - someone to share sunsets
- An archivist - someone who remembers you way back when
- A friendly competitor - someone who raises the stakes for you to keep up with
- A creative catalyst - someone who brings out your most original self
- A health helper - someone with whom you enjoy exercising and sharing healthy habits
- A colleague - someone who helps you operate at your best and contribute at your highest
- A partner - someone who shares commitment and connection over time
- A family - people who share a past, a present and a future lovingly

Streamlining your structure is about three things:
What do I want?
What can I let go of?
What will I hold on to?

CHAPTER SIX

Applications, Variations & Inspirations

THE DEEPER QUIET

Have you ever been half-awake
lying in bed in the dark
listening to night's peacefulness,
and then,

just when you are full of comfortable quiet,
some appliance or household system cuts off
and a new level of stillness descends
gently,
deepening the night.

So this new level of quiet reminds you
how accustomed you are to some perpetual
noise.
How blunted you are by the daily din.

As you look at blending
success and satisfaction,
as you reflect in quiet moments
on what matters,
you may enjoy visiting some thoughts,
some joys, some sorrows, some textures,
some glimpses of times when you have...

> Tasted the moment
> Shaped the meaning
> Held the mission

And from such remembered glimpses,
of laughter, of love, of realities,
may you take away refreshment,
some glow to light the way to tomorrow.

As you work your way through the 28-day plan, you might enjoy the following selections.

Two are reprints from **DELIGHTS, DILEMMAS, DECISIONS:** *The Gift of Living Lightly.* Most are new. You might even begin writing your own. You could start an annual notebook with words and images to capture the highlights of your year. Notice that most of these selections overlap or blend the three principles of Taste, Shape, Hold.

Each of these is a complete short selection. Sample them anytime.

THE GLASS HALF...

Alexandria at one. She is all energy, warmth and wetness. Even when her diaper is dry, she's dribbling her apple juice, splashing her bath water, or drooling on my shoulder in an instant nap. She's a wet kid.

She's just at that stage of pulling herself up, bouncing on her legs while keeping a tight grip on the coffee table and getting ready to walk. She's about one step away from her first step.

She still drinks from the cup-with-a-cap we give kids. So, of course, she is enthralled with the half-glass of water that I, her untrained great-aunt, just set down on the coffee table. She stares fixedly at the clear glass, the clear liquid. Water—an opportunity for wet!

She gets herself within grabbing distance of the glass and does something wonderful. She leaves the glass safely on the table and sticks her whole face, nose and tongue into the glass—and she can't get the water. She backs away and studies the glass.

Now she takes it in her hands and again sticks her face, nose and tongue in. On this particular morning it doesn't yet occur to her to tilt the glass and let the water come to her. I know this is a tiny moment in Alexandria's childhood. Tomorrow she will figure out how to tilt the glass and cascade water all down herself.

And here's what she helped me wonder about in that moment. What if I am God's 1-year old. What if the glass is in front of me, waiting, more than half full? And I keep reaching after it with my face instead of letting it flow to me.

I want to control the glass. I want to figure out on my own how to get the water. I want to invent a straw and know I did it on my own. And the water just sits there. Waiting for me to accept it.

Alexandria's good news is that once she "gets it," she knows the secret of the water forever. My good news. Even after I learn to let go and accept the flow I will still forget regularly and get to be amused at being God's 1-year old all my life.

And the water just sits there.

Waiting for me to accept it.

I'VE ONLY RUN OUT OF GAS TWICE IN MY LIFE

Running out of gas feels stupid. How much trouble can it be to check the gas gauge and make sure there is fuel in the tank?

I remember that morning with embarrassing vividness. I was heading north on Georgia Avenue near a shopping center. An odd sound escaped from the car which shuddered gradually but jerkily to a coasting roll. Even though I had never run out of gas before, I diagnosed my problem instantly. Fortunately it was a suburban street, not rush hour, in an easy place to pull over, not too far from a gas station. Everything was working for me this time. Still I bristled at being in such a predicament. It was tempting to blame it on the men in my life.

When my gas gauge stopped working my engineer husband and son knew exactly what to do. "You don't have to fix it," they said, "just remember to always fill the tank to the top and reset your odometer. You can go about 350 miles on one tank and you'll know when to refill." What I didn't know was that my son had borrowed my car while I was away on business. He stopped for gas and didn't have quite enough money to fill the tank. He reset the odometer anyway.

I recovered from the first experience and the odometer solution was working again. Until that morning on the beltway in rush hour. This time I was zipping along in the far left lane, passing the trucks which are forbidden from driving in the "fast" lane. This time when the engine coughed pitifully and started to shudder I was stricken with panic. "I'll never get this baby off the road." I crept across three lanes, humbled now that the trucks were courteously letting me over. I got to the side and someone stopped to help. Lucky again.

And this story has very little to do with gas tanks, and everything to do with the concept of "finite resources."

Gas is a finite resource. The car must have gasoline to operate. It doesn't matter how powerful or persuasive I am. It doesn't matter whether I am rushing to close a million dollar deal or to take Mother Theresa to the hospital. It doesn't matter whether I intended to get gas later or whether I am going to feed it premium if it could only help me through this small crunch right now. Gas is finite. Gas is nonnegotiable.

And we are like that car. Our gas gauges are sometimes broken. We sometimes don't know when we must have more sleep, more food, more joy, more love, more challenge, more learning. We don't always see the finite nature of life itself.

ONCE, IN A STORE,
IN INDIANA

It was the summer I was back home
to take care of Dad.

One day I had time to go downtown
and revisit the legendary department stores--
the retail giants of my childhood,
Aldens, Roots, Meis, Wards and Penny's--
all in a row on Wabash Avenue.

At the cosmetics counter in Roots
a face greeted me,
faintly floating back into focus
from my high school yearbook.

"Hi! Where have you been for the last 10
years?" she asked.

"I'm here from Washington,
visiting my folks," I answered

"What do you do now?"

And for a moment
I couldn't remember.
I was in a time so full
of caring for a parent,
of revisiting my school memories,
of retasting the past,
that I went entirely blank
about what I did,
or who I was
today.

It was a moment of freedom
that has only ever happened to me

once, in a store, in Indiana.

THE SLAVE OF VELCRO

Until my early 40's, my idea of a perfect day off was to lie on a cozy couch, dressed in a bathrobe, cuddled in a blanket, sipping a fragrant cup of tea and reading a murder mystery. No phone, no kids, no errands, no interruptions.

One day my aerobics-teaching sister and my weightlifting stepson kidnapped me and dragged me to a mall. I hate malls. I hate spending money. But there's something I love—Velcro. I love how velcro works every time. I love that nobody ever sends me a card offering to upgrade my velcro. I've never seen a velcro recall like they do with cars. Velcro just works every time. I even love the sound.

They made me try on some exercise shoes with velcro. I fell in love with the velcro and had to buy the shoes. I bought the shoes, went home, put the shoes on and stretched out on the couch. (The shoes stayed very clean.)

"No, Mag," they said, "those shoes like to go outside." Reluctantly I took the shoes outside. We went to the corner and back. My feet started to like that. Eventually they got the rest of my body to like it too. Now I walk at least 20 miles a week or I feel diminished. I'm so addicted that if I don't work up a good exercise sweat, I don't feel like I deserve the hot water for a shower.

Like a lot of other people, I used to feel I didn't have time for exercise. What I learned is that exercise gives me back a lot of time—in clearer thinking, in fewer mistakes, in resistance to colds, in the extra vitality I bring to all my day.

Now I don't have time **not** to exercise. I love the symphony of muscles, brain and bones. I find fresh air an aphrodisiac inviting me to fall in love with my life each day.

And I still get an occasional moment to revel in a visit to that cozy couch. After grand effort, great ease.

After grand effort...

Great ease.

THE SONG OF THE SEATBELT

While my stepson was in college we learned the truth of the bumper stickers that say "MY KID AND MY MONEY GO TO VIRGINIA TECH." Eventually, after five long years, he graduated with his electrical engineering degree, and having no money, no job, and no place else to live--promptly moved back home with us.

Household patterns shifted and now he was the one on that cozy couch when I came home from work. We started out asking how the job search was going. One day he said to me "Aw, Mag, you know how I can't stand to be rejected." I was so impressed that an engineer talked about feelings that I left him alone for a while.

One day he came bursting in with, "Dad, Mag, I've got great news."
"Wow, you got a job?" we asked.
"No, I joined a health club."

Eventually, of course, he did get a job. His dad and I both rearranged our schedules to watch him leave on that first day of work.

He looked great. New charcoal grey suit, fresh haircut, tilted smile, and his dad's red silk tie. The tie did it. It brought back his first day of kindergarten, his little red lunchbox and the band-aid on his knee all those years ago. This morning is another launch.

We all hug and he crosses over and gets into his shiny red car. He is about to drive off and start a new level of self-sufficiency. As we stand there feeling all those complex parental feelings, he closes his car door, reaches up to his shoulder harness, pulls the seatbelt across himself, and he clicks it into place with a loud metallic click.

Suddenly, inside that "click," I hear lots of things most of us rarely hear. I hear, "Thanks for my education." I hear "I'm going off today, but I take with me more than you even remember teaching me." I hear "I'm taking care of myself so we have long lives to share together."

I think of that moment now as "the song of the seatbelt" Such simple, subtle reminders let me know that what I do is important. That I teach more than I know. That I am loved, valued and appreciated. I listen for the song of the seatbelt in the ordinary music of each day.

I listen for the Song of the Seatbelt in the ordinary music of each day.

THE BRENDA BONUS

I can almost tell you the exact moment I fell in love with my prospective daughter-in-law.

We knew that this girl was special from the beginning because Chuck was living with us when they met. We saw subtle changes in him immediately. Then there was the first time she was coming to the house and he worked six hours to clean the abandoned hot tub so they could enjoy it together.

Brenda arrived. Cool, blonde and brittle. She was wonderfully nice in a distant sort of way. And Marty and I stayed out of the path of the young couple.

For the next few months we saw them occasionally when she came over for a football game or a bike ride. She fixed some mean chipdips and ate warmed, buttered brie by the wheel. All this without a blemish on her fresh-from-the-gym figure.

We were increasingly charmed by this accountant from Jackson, Mississippi. She won the hearts of Chuck's young cousins, Alexandra and Gabriella, at Easter, and gruff Uncle Harry gifted her with a piece of his pottery.

The relationship was getting serious. Then Chuck was transferred to Italy for three months.

He called at 11:30 one night—5:30 a.m. his time. "Dad, I need your help. Brenda is over in the townhouse she shares with Connie who is out of town. Connie and her boyfriend had an argument just before she left town...and now the boyfriend has come into the townhouse and he is in Connie's room making noises with the door closed. Brenda is frightened and she's coming over to spend the night with you guys. She'll be there in about 20 minutes."

We put the porch light on, hastily made a "Welcome, Brenda" sign and put it on the front door. A few minutes later she drove up and we went out to meet her. Marty took her small overnight case and we walked her inside. Once inside, I gave her a hug, pulled away and noticed the tears in her eyes. Here was that rock-solid professional woman showing a glimpse of the fragile, frightened child in each of us.

I knew I loved her, the whole package. Her competence and her frailty, her charm and her independence, her polish, her power and her vulnerability. Standing in that narrow hallway on Great Oak Road on one night in September, I welcomed a new daughter into my family.

GRIEF IS A FUNNY THING

Grief comes in many forms as a result of many kinds of losses. After a death, after breaking up a marriage or relationship, after getting fired, after a loss of money, health, self-respect or innocence.

Three of my responses to grief were easy to predict, two were surprising.

After two of my brothers died, I learned to accept the waves of sorrow and loss that came up unexpectedly. These waves were totally engulfing and might hit while I was in a checkout line at the store or when I woke up in the dark. While each wave caught me off guard, I wasn't surprised at the whole idea of them.

The second response relates to the odd logic of loss. Immediately after major losses I've known, I welcome bonding and support from other people to get me over the shock. After a short while, though, I notice that I hold people at increasingly greater distances. Death is such an enormous desertion. It is the ultimate rejection.

Some reptile logic deep in my unconscious mind triggers this rejection pattern. "My Mom loved me, yet she deserted me; my husband loves me, he will desert me too, so I might as well withdraw now."

You can fill in any names in the formula. It makes sense at a primitive level. It's just not a satisfying way to live. Once I noticed this response, it didn't surprise me either.

The third response is total vulnerability to the smallest sensory triggers: the smell of apple pie, a whiff of smoke from a fireplace, a commercial for one brand of car, a news item about a similar death, a travel poster from a place we vacationed, a glance between strangers in an elevator, a song on the radio, a favorite old movie on TV, the first robin of spring, the taste of hazelnut coffee, the sight of a favorite sweater that was handed down to one of the kids, a half-familiar voice on the phone--all of these moments can put a violent boot in my belly or a sweet recall in my heart and pull me completely out of today.

The first of the surprising responses was the unpredictability of a whole range of skills that I usually enjoy taking for granted.

I discovered that I can still perform all basic functions while grieving. I can operate, show up, drive, work, do errands, get groceries. These are the functions of Range 1.

I also can operate in Range 3, where I reflect, consider meanings of things, think long term, and create/revise my perspective on life.

Range 2 is the area that goes all unpredict-able. Sometimes it works just fine, and the next moment it is totally missing. Range 2 includes decision-making, judgment, and lots of stored information. When Range 2 goes dark, I can't remember a phone number I call every day; I can't focus on a menu long enough to remember what I like to order; I can't select the best strategy to get me to a goal; I don't know how to drive somewhere familiar; I forget that a nearby street became one-way five years ago; I don't remember what brand of toothpaste to buy.

The worst part about these lapses is that I outwardly seem to be fine. I've even convinced myself that things are back to normal. But they're not. Maybe all the cultures which have traditions about wearing special clothing during mourning are wise. Maybe it would be good to alert myself and others to the fact that I'm not all here.

I think that I'm putting all of my unconscious energy into Range 3, so that I have no resources left to handle items in Range 2.

The other surprising part about grief is that sometimes it leaks away gradually, and sometimes it is lifted in a single moment. I was in my 30's when my Father died. His was the first death in my nuclear family. He had a long and eventful life, raised a prospering family, and died one week after the whole family gathered to celebrate his and Mom's 50th wedding anniversary.

That first year without him was tough. I responded to grief by keeping people at a distance. I was also very concerned for Mom. My husband and I called her about three months after Daddy died and proposed a trip to their birthplace in Ireland for the following summer. Thus I ended up hiking a hillside in Ireland almost exactly one year after daddy's death.

It was a brilliant sunny summer day, rare in Ireland. The hillside was a moving sea of knee-high grasses bending and flowing with gusty breezes. I paused at the hilltop to look down at a view of the diamond-sparkling sea, the small village, the cattle grazing on the next hill, full-bodied clouds floating above, a giant boulder to sit on for a moment, my patient husband hiking nearby.

And in that single moment, surrounded by the glorious beauty and abundance of a home I had never seen before, and grace beyond my asking, my grief was lifted. It was almost like a hiccup leaving me. There was a lurch of letting something go inside my stomach and a immediate lift as if my heart were a balloon caught up in that hillside's mighty breeze.

It's not that I didn't continue to think of Daddy. It's just that after that single moment, the thought held more of light and joy than of loss or pain. There have been few transform-ing moments in my life, but that was truly one.

UNEXPECTED COMFORTS

Do you ever feel at a loss in comforting someone after a death? I find that even sending a
condolence card can be tough, because I don't
know what to write in it and I worry that just a
signature isn't enough.

I realized after my Mother died that I appreciated everything people offered in the way of
support—including cards with just signatures.

One comment in a card, though, especially
stirred me. "I never met your Mother, but I
can tell that you probably carry some of her
qualities. When I see your love of books and
your gift for sensing people's feelings I wonder
if those are your legacy from her."

Another action amazed me. I was in the
middle of a big project and needed some disks
printed on a high-resolution printer. A service
vendor with whom I had worked once before
agreed to do the job and have it ready when I
got back from the funeral in Indiana. I picked
up the job and asked Cathy for the invoice.

"There won't be an invoice. You see, I just got
this printer brand new. This is the first job I
have done on it. I want you to take this as my
thanks for the blessing of a new printer and as
my way of offering comfort in the way most
available to me now." I could hardly drive
away through the tear-blur of feeling cher-
ished, supported and touched by strangers.

That is one of the most moving gestures anyone has ever offered me.

May I remember to offer comfort in the way most available to me now.

ONE MORE GIFT

I had never touched a dead person before.

I had no intention of touching Mom in the casket. But my brother Conn reached over and covered her freckled hand with his own. He spoke directly to the still, stiff face. He spoke with reverence, with love, with remembered laughter, patting her on the hand as I'd see him do so often at the nursing home.

And when it came time for me to kneel there alone, I reached across to touch her, too. And got one more gift. It wasn't her. It was a shell. A beautiful shell like the statues we used to pray to in church. It was an empty container. My Mom was surely gone—to Daddy, to Auntie, to Winnie, Nora, Dell, Frank and Moe. We were the ones left behind. Waiting.

The trip to the cemetery was anticlimactic. "This isn't mom," I thought, "this is just the empty container."

She still had that to teach me at her funeral.

LISTENING

I sit outside on a Saturday morning
late in August.

Cicadas chirp the deep musical undertone
of summer on the east coast,
while jets hum far, far overhead.

A light breeze blesses the air,
and fills the flags above.
Summer is making a graceful exit for a change.

Earlier this morning the geese honked their
way across the pearl grey sky,
pulling September ever closer in their echoes.

Now church bells surprise me
with unexpected morning music,
celebrating a nearby wedding.

Summer's song fades.
A community grows
in the joy of wedding bells.

The ebb and flow of eternity
is all around me.

There to notice
if only I
listen.

YOUR SILENCES

I have made a collection of your silences:

> ...your sleeping silence, cuddled in the
> bedclothes in a cold house,

> ...the quiet of your concentration over
> the checkbook,

> ...the moment that our eyes meet over
> early morning coffee,

> ...the seconds before you told me that
> my brother had died,

> ...the sweet silence after sex.

I have made a collection of your silences
to play back when I am missing you.

ON OUR 20TH WEDDING ANNIVERSARY

Marriage is one of several arrangements that helps adults live full, rich lives. Yes, I smile when someone defines bigamy as having one spouse too many and monogamy as being the same thing. I think of marriage as a lifetime communication adventure.

One day on our walk, I told Marty I was thinking of taking up painting. He glanced at me without missing a stride and asked, "semigloss or latex?"

Wrestling with the idea of this 20th anniversary, I thought about the long-ago magic of being new in a relationship. Meeting someone new, finding things in common, a first date, first touch, first kiss, first snuggle, first everything. It's odd that I remember it all so warmly, because I usually hated these things when I was going through them. I continued my daydream about the new times, a wedding trousseau, all new underwear, champagne kisses.

One morning, my well-worn husband and I were up early taking our customary walk of about four miles. We usually turn around at the two-mile point in a shady spot where two cedar trees create a natural secluded private arch above us. Often we kiss there.

This particular day, as I was thinking about all the "new" things I was missing out on, his kiss almost caught me by surprise.

And there in the middle of a hot, sticky, sweaty exercise-panting kiss I was flooded with the cumulative gift of twenty years. We had been together through the deaths of three parents and two brothers. We had seen his son graduate from Virginia Tech. We had camped from Nova Scotia to the Canadian Rockies. We had shared songs with my family in Ireland one Fourth of July and we had hiked along the Bay in Anchorage, Alaska. We had shared a lot of potatoes, a lot of sunrises and a lot of life.

Finally, the resonance of all that life had its own kind of newness. I had never before celebrated this level of sharing with another human being. This moment was new.

Inside our oldest commitments can lie our newest celebrations.

AFTERWARD:
THREE QUESTIONS TO SUMMARIZE

QUESTION 1
This is fine. The book is helpful. But I'm in a hurry. If there were only one thing I could do today to have more success and satisfaction, what would that one thing be?

ANSWER
Make a date with yourself and keep it. Give yourself one hour today to think about your life. How to have more what you really want. You can never lie to yourself, but you can stay deaf for a very long time. We call this denial. What is it you are pretending not to hear in your life? Eventually the truth leaks out in health or performance. Remember what C. S. Lewis said: "Pain is God's megaphone to the deaf."

QUESTION 2
What, specifically, would I do in that hour?

ANSWER
Why not get an ice cream cone, or a slice of crispy bread, or an apple? Think about the three principles:

> Taste the Moment
> Shape the Meaning
> Hold the Mission.

Savor that taste of whatever you are eating. Can you taste the separate molecules? Slow down until they come to you. Once you can taste the molecules you will more easily taste the moment. Once you can taste the moment you will have the gift of Noticing Ordinary Wonders. Once you have the gift of NOW you are indeed blending success and satisfacton.

My best exercise each day is to shiver with delight at my place in life.
Conn McAuliffe

QUESTION 3
I'm fine when I'm focused on this subject. But the minute I forget to watch my thoughts, my brain wanders back to the hurrying habit. Any suggestions for how I can stay more aware and quiet the To-Do list in my head?

ANSWER
Use the 5 X 5 FORMULA for daily success and satisfaction.

You can practice this easy mental exercise each day. Bring your mind to this formula any time you aren't sure what to think about.

Take one word from column 1 one from column 3. Use any preposition from column 2 to link your statement.

LOVE	for	YOURSELF
LAUGH	with	FAMILY
LEARN	from	BUSINESS
LINK	with	OTHERS
LISTEN	to	GOD

Loop around in the formula and go where your thoughts take you. You can't go far wrong!

YOUR SUCCESS/ SATISFACTION INDEX

This **LIFE BALANCE INVENTORY** helps you assess where you are now and where you would prefer to be in seven zones of life.

On each of the following items, circle the number that reflects where you are today. Star the number that reflects where you prefer to be. Don't assume that you must want to be a "10" on every item. Shape your own definitions.

This helps you develop a personalized profile of how success and satisfaction would look in your life today, not in some abstract model of perfection that would appy all the time.

1. I sleep easily and awake refreshed.
   1 2 3 4 5 6 7 8 9 10
2. I eat the variety and amount of food that helps me feel nourished and alert.
   1 2 3 4 5 6 7 8 9 10
3. I am pleased with my overall appearance.
   1 2 3 4 5 6 7 8 9 10
4. I have enough energy to reach my goals.
   1 2 3 4 5 6 7 8 9 10
5. I exercise regularly and enjoyably.
   1 2 3 4 5 6 7 8 9 10
6. I avoid excesses of salt, sugar, tobacco, alcohol and caffeine.
   1 2 3 4 5 6 7 8 9 10

7. I spend as much time as I want with my
   spouse/partner.
      1 2 3 4 5 6 7 8 9 10

8. I spend as much time as I want with other
   family members.
      1 2 3 4 5 6 7 8 9 10

9. The time I spend with family refreshes and
   restores me.
      1 2 3 4 5 6 7 8 9 10

10. Family communication is satisfying.
      1 2 3 4 5 6 7 8 9 10

11. Family members share past memories,
   present challenges and future visions and
   goals.
      1 2 3 4 5 6 7 8 9 10

12. Belonging to this family is of great value
   to me.
      1 2 3 4 5 6 7 8 9 10

13. My financial affairs, retirement and estate
   plans are in order.
      1 2 3 4 5 6 7 8 9 10

14. I have a will which reflects current realities
   and responsibilities.
      1 2 3 4 5 6 7 8 9 10

15. I have the money to do the things that
   are important to me.
      1 2 3 4 5 6 7 8 9 10

16. I rarely worry about money.
      1 2 3 4 5 6 7 8 9 10

17. I am happy to give money, gifts or
   donations when I want.
      1 2 3 4 5 6 7 8 9 10

18. I feel prosperous.
      1 2 3 4 5 6 7 8 9 10

19. My career is challenging
     1 2 3 4 5 6 7 8 9 10
20. I am recognized and rewarded for my work
     1 2 3 4 5 6 7 8 9 10
21. What I do is important.
     1 2 3 4 5 6 7 8 9 10
22. I have the mental, physical, and financial
    resources to get my job done.
     1 2 3 4 5 6 7 8 9 10
23. What I do makes a difference.
     1 2 3 4 5 6 7 8 9 10
24. Work gives me a strong sense of
    accomplishment.
     1 2 3 4 5 6 7 8 9 10
25. I am a contributor to my community,
    nation, world.
     1 2 3 4 5 6 7 8 9 10
26. I participate in professional, church, school
    and/or community groups.
     1 2 3 4 5 6 7 8 9 10
27. I donate time/money to issues I believe in.
     1 2 3 4 5 6 7 8 9 10
28. I participate in the political process.
     1 2 3 4 5 6 7 8 9 10
29. I stay informed on global issues.
     1 2 3 4 5 6 7 8 9 10
30. I am proud of my participation in my
    community/world.
     1 2 3 4 5 6 7 8 9 10
31. I am comfortable with my views on what
    happens after death.
     1 2 3 4 5 6 7 8 9 10
32. I believe my life has meaning--I make a
    contribution.
     1 2 3 4 5 6 7 8 9 10

33. I operate consistently within my personal sense of honesty and ethics.
1 2 3 4 5 6 7 8 9 10
34. I have a clear sense of the role God (my higher power) plays in my life.
1 2 3 4 5 6 7 8 9 10
35. Shared spiritual values strengthen my relationships.
1 2 3 4 5 6 7 8 9 10
36. I dedicate time regularly to my spiritual needs.
1 2 3 4 5 6 7 8 9 10
37. I have time to myself regularly.
1 2 3 4 5 6 7 8 9 10
38. I have time for things that are important to me.
1 2 3 4 5 6 7 8 9 10
39. I have a keen sense of humor.
1 2 3 4 5 6 7 8 9 10
40. I communicate effectively.
1 2 3 4 5 6 7 8 9 10
41. I rarely feel guilty or resentful.
1 2 3 4 5 6 7 8 9 10
42. I am comfortable with who I am.
1 2 3 4 5 6 7 8 9 10

1. Total the numbers in all your circles.   _____

2. Total the numbers in all your stars.   _____

3. Subtract the circles' number from the stars' number.   _____

This equals your success-satisfaction gap.
  0-50 shows exceptional balance
  51-150 shows average balance
  151+ shows strained balance
In deciding where to start to improve the quality of your life, choose the items from this list which mean the most to you.

QUESTIONS PARTICIPANTS ASK ABOUT THE INVENTORY

QUESTION:
Why wouldn't I want to be a 10 on every item?

ANSWER:
You develop your own personal profile of preferred balance in your life. This lets you evaluate choices.

If you are starting a new business, getting a degree or having a baby you may elect to give up some sleep. If this is your freely chosen option, it is less of a strain on you than if you are required to work overtime every day for five months.

You can't deny physical needs, like sleep, forever, but free choice lightens any load.

If you are hitting a snag in your career, you may want to drop back on your expectations in this area temporarily. There are times when survival is a more appropriate focus than satisfaction.

QUESTION:
Should I take the LIFE BALANCE INVENTORY more than once?

ANSWER:
This can be a helpful tool to review periodically. Your answers may not change in a single

year, or they may. Some program participants have their spouse complete an inventory too. They talk about their answers and use them to set shared goals.

QUESTION:
What are the life zones reflected in the LBI?

ANSWER:
The 42 items in the inventory are divided as follows:

Items 1-6	Health
Items 7-12	Family
Items 13-18	Finance
Items 19-24	Career
Items 25-30	Community
Items 31-36	Spirit
Items 37-42	Self

You might look back at your answers and draw a line between each section above.

This can help you see the area where you are the strongest and the area you may want to improve first.

THE INSPIRATONAL INVITATIONAL

Here's a challenge. Once a year, why not let me know you are out there. Let me know how you are using what you read. What you'd like to hear more about in coming books. Win a prize!

Thus, the annual Inspirational Invitational

Each Invitational starts from right now to just before Thanksgiving each year. Entries must be postmarked or FAXed by November 15, and winners will be announced January 3 of the following year. 5 winners a year get the top prize of $50 credit from the BCI Press catalog which features books, tapes, cards, T-shirts, jewelry and novelty items. Obviously, you are doing this for the challenge and not for rampant greed!

Contests calling for drawings will not be judged on artistic merit. They will be judged on how effectively your sketch, drawing, icon or stick figure conveys a message with impact.

Feel free to use whimsy, humor, science, tecnology, cutouts, clip-art, creativity and flair! Each entry may include 50 words or less about your entry or the concept for the year.

Judges each year are impartial associates of BCI Press. They include selected specialists from:

- National Geographic Photographers
- Award-winning advertising firms
- CEO's of entrepreneurial firms
- Specialists at visual impact
- Authors of bestselling books

People involved in BCI Press and the judging associates are excluded from competition.

Here are the topics for coming years:

TOPIC	DEADLINE
Design an international symbol for "Contentment"	Nov. 15, 1995

What does contentment look like? What are the visual elements? Is the symbol spare or rich with symbols? What colors do you see?

Create your bumper sticker with or without an icon	Nov. 15, 1996

What is your 25-word-or-less mission statement or bumper sticker? If you had a personal logo/icon, what would it be?

Sketch your family/life crest	Nov. 15, 1997

Is your crest shaped more like a coat of arms or a stained glass window? What symbols or elements appear? Any words or slogans?

All entries become property of BCI Press, so keep a copy for yourself. If you would like an announcement of the winner and honorable mentions, include a stamped, self-addressed business-sized envelope with your entry.

This book is part of a continuing conversation I love having with idea explorers. Join in!

ORDER BLANK

*Contact BCI Press for information
on substantial discounts on quantity orders of any
of our selections.
Call 301-460-3408 or FAX 301-871-7225*

SPEAK LIKE A PRO: A Business Tool for Marketing & Managing (BCI Press)
A fresh, focused and functional guide for improving your impact in speeches, at meetings and on television. Includes the Emergency 10-minutes-to-prepare Panic Plan and the Speaking Skill Development Inventory.
$25+$4 S/H (MD residents please add sales tax)

DELIGHTS, DILEMMAS, DECISIONS:The Gift of Living Lightly (KIT Publishers)
When relaxation and balance are high on your To-Do list, here's help and hope. Explore life's 7 areas and practice small sanities to keep your perspective amid the daily drain.
$20 +$4 S/H (MD residents please add sales tax)

LIFE IS MORE THAN YOUR TO-DO LIST: Blending Business Success With Personal Satisfaction (BCI Press)
Would you like to wake up tomorrow brimming with a sense of vibrant possibilities? This practical guide offers a 28-day program to producing more rich, relaxed results each day.
$12.95+$4 S/H (MD residents please add sales tax)

*For information on Maggie Bedrosian as a speaker
or executive coach, please contact*
Maggie Bedrosian, c/o
BCI Press • 4509 Great Oak Rd. • Rockville, MD 20853
Voice - 301•460•3408 FAX - 301•871•7225

```
SHIP TO:
Name
Address


Autograph to:
Total Enclosed:
```